Westergasfabriek Culture Park

Transformation of a former industrial site in Amsterdam

Olof Koekebakker

Westergasfabriek Culture Park

Transformation of a former industrial site in Amsterdam

NAi Publishers

Content

Brownfield passages
From Westergasfabriek to the New Westerpark

The central work of civil societies in the first part of the twenty-first century will be to address the legacy of industrialization from previous centuries. For many cities, municipalities and communities this work is concerned with the reclamation and reuse of brownfield sites that by virtue of their past industrial production uses, are now physically degraded, environmentally disturbed, and chemically contaminated. Or more significantly for all those involved in the shaping of our urban environments it is the passage of these brownfield lands from dereliction and pollution to culturally energetic and socially sustainable creative centers that thrusts these formerly discounted lands into becoming vital agents of change. The productive life of factories, manufacturing plants and industrial production fully comes to an end, and is replaced by abandonment and dereliction. This brownfield site indicates not just a change in physical appearance or a simple return to the productive use of exhausted and currently undervalued plots of ground – a tidying up of the past industrial environment. Rather it signals a profound shift in the way in which we must lay claim to this disputed area. Disputed because it is still a highly contentious part of our late twentieth century landscape, through its association with the by-products of heavy industrialization (empty buildings, the infrastructure of canals, rails and storage, waste, toxic soils and groundwater) long after these processes have ceased. The subject of reclaiming and recycling derelict or contaminated brownfield land therefore exerts a special fascination today that is not fully explained by the influence it has on the planning and rebuilding of city neighborhoods. Governments, cities and private industry will commit billions of dollars annually to clean up sites like Westergasfabriek contaminated with hazardous waste and toxic materials. Arising from this the following questions loom large on the horizon:
•	How do brownfield sites like Westergasfabriek shape national landscapes and future communities, towns and regions?
•	How do these brownfield lands structure the changing needs of scientific and aesthetic knowledge?
How does the restoration, recycling, and redevelopment of sites such as decommissioned manufacturing plants, derelict urban waterfronts, inner city factories affect how the public will perceive and interact with the natural and manmade world in the 21st century?
•	In this regard the former Westergasfabriek site stands as an exemplary project and intense international attention is now focused on the New Westerpark site reclamation and reoccupation as a model for efforts in other urban centers around the world.

This recognition is perhaps best explained through three areas of endeavor over the life of this project so far. The first can be directed to the initial perceptions

by a variety of stakeholders, residents and city officials of the enormous ongo-
ing cultural, social and civic value of the Westergasfabriek site even in its former
physical state. Not only perceptions but the transformation of these opinions
and thoughts into a series of clear and directed actions about the interim
inhabitation of the landscape and the increasing visibility of the site in the
urban social fabric. In this the Westergasfabriek points to the temporary inhabitation in the physical structure of a brownfield site as a working method for
other communities and cities to recapture the values of their lost or vacant
lands. The second is in the development of a consistent and creative vision for
the site that at the same time is robust yet flexible over time and embraces all
stakeholders and local communities. In this regard, Westergasfabriek through
the consistent reinforcement of the initial vision in all forms of media and activities demonstrates for other agencies and countries the seriousness of the act of
brownfield reclamation as a social and cultural endeavor as well as the merits
of focused attention on the day to day. Finally the areas of endeavor associated
with the physical, social and material qualities of the site continue to be underscored on the Westergasfabriek project. In short in contemporary urban life
there is a constant struggle against the fake, the replica, and the lack of authen-
ticity – or more importantly an eager searching for the real and the vital in civic
endeavors. The Westergasfabriek project by folding historic surfaces, structures
and places with emerging and progressive ideas in green open space, gives
direction to other brownfield communities in the need to protect and enhance
the visceral qualities of modern cities in another step in their evolution.

To introduce the subject of brownfield reclamation, it must first be noted that
one of the seemingly inevitable consequences of industrialization processes is
the production of land that remains despoiled, in one manner or another, long
after the occupants have moved on. Many major cities, industrial towns and
rural communities have as part of their built fabric – abandoned railroad yards,
obsolete manufacturing gas plants, disused factories, exhausted and closed
landfill sites, and other brownfield lands often in valuable locations for future
use, adjacent to centers of population. Moreover, as the economic, social, cultural, ecological and other potentials of these sites become more fully recognized, new projects and uses are proposed, plans for redevelopment are drawn
up, and methods are sought to clean up the despoiled sites, returning them
once again to potentially productive use. This is both a new and an old activity,
and one that has certainly caught the attention of regulators, designers, developers, engineers, lawyers and planners in many parts of the world. It is old
because the process of recycling land (or in the case of the Netherlands the
making of land from scratch) has been going on since antiquity. It is new
because of the relative magnitude and exotic nature of the pollutants involved
today, and therefore, the remediation technologies, interdisciplinary design
strategies and creative programs required for rectification and reuse. In addi-

tion it involves a greater number of stakeholders and other interested parties than ever before. This in turn has led to sometimes contentious debate about the future of these sites and has created rifts between those who support development or preservation, ecology or commerce, cities or neighborhoods, arts or business, private or public.

For the public and professional viewer therefore the New Westerpark offers a glimpse into the considerable influence of addressing – together and holistically – current social, environmental and community issues encountered in such an undertaking. In addition it communicates technological issues of reclamation and renewal and dispels myths surrounding the limiting factors brought about by the toxic nature of degraded brownfield sites. Finally by presenting such a clear example of the passage from conceptual design ideas to implemented built work, it stimulates both professional and public dialogue concerning the range of possibilities that may exist for such sites in the future around the world.

Niall Kirkwood is Professor of Landscape Architecture and Technology and Chair of the Department of Landscape Architecture at the Harvard Graduate School of Design, Cambridge, MA, USA.

The metamorphos

When the Netherlands changed over to natural gas in the early nineteen sixties, the old coal-gas production facilities shut down one by one. The same fate was reserved for the Westergasfabriek, a large gasworks at the western edge of the inner city of Amsterdam. The buildings on the site also became redundant. That most of them were spared from demolition was not due to their noteworthy architecture (which, remarkably enough, nobody noticed until much later) but because it was easy to adapt them for new functions such as storage.

The complex nonetheless kept its old name, Westergasfabriek ('West Gas Factory'). It is a name that is now better known to the average Amsterdam resident than ever before – better indeed than in the days, over forty years ago, when the plant still supplied coal gas to the city. It acquired this reputation in the early nineties, after the urban district of Westerpark assigned the former gasworks for use for cultural activities. Since then, thousands of visitors from Amsterdam and elsewhere have attended a wide variety of events at the Westergasfabriek, ranging from theatre productions to art fairs, from circuses to house parties, and from fashion shows to company festivities.

The surroundings of the buildings have meanwhile undergone a complete metamorphosis. A new park has been laid out on the 14.5 hectare grounds to a design by the American landscape architect Kathryn Gustafson. Now it is the turn of the buildings, which are in the process of a comprehensive renovation to restore them to their former splendour. Still, things were remarkably quiet in the Westergasfabriek for a period. The soil decontamination programme made most of the site inaccessible to the public. But it looks like the Westergasfabriek will once again become a hive of cultural activity in the foreseeable future.

The transformation of the Westergasfabriek was, and still is, an enterprise of huge complexity, a parallel chess-match on many boards. From the moment the new designated function was decided, it was necessary to continually readjust the plans for the park, the buildings and the soil-cleaning operation to one another. Moreover, different players were (and still are) playing at all those boards. The main ones are the Westerpark district council (initiator and client for the park creation and the soil cleaning) and the real estate development company MAB, which has taken the buildings over from the district council to convert them to their future functions. Other principle players are the designers of the plans, the contractors carrying them out, the central city authorities, the residents of the adjoining neighbourhoods and the cultural

Construction of the new park,
May 2003

s of a gasworks

companies and organizations who use the buildings on an incidental or permanent basis.

There are no books of instructions or recipes for long, complicated operations like these. It is an illusion to think the necessary process can be set down in straightforward terms, because there are too many uncertain factors. This is not to say the process is uncontrollable; however, instead of a concrete end-position, the course has to be determined by a vision set out in broad lines, and by a concept of what can be achieved based on that vision. The first exertions

thus consisted mainly of hammering out the vision and the concept, which were subsequently to guide all the activities involved in bringing the transformation of the Westergasfabriek to a good conclusion.

The new Westergasfabriek resists description in a single term; it is many things at the same time. Its huge diversity is indeed on of its most distinctive features. For a start, the Westergasfabriek is, as said, a new park in an urban district that has never been generously endowed with greenery. Strictly speaking, it is a contemporary extension to the nineteenth-century public park that gave the district its name, Westerpark, lying to the east of the Westergasfabriek. The old park was too small from the outset, being the only green area within reach for tens of thousands of Amsterdam residents. Now, after more than a century, the Westerpark has finally gained the size people originally had in mind for it in the nineteenth century – before there was any suggestion of a gasworks. The park is primarily an amenity for the neighbourhoods Spaarndammerbuurt and Staatsliedenbuurt, but the events that occur there will be for the benefit of people from all over Amsterdam and sometimes far beyond. The main location for the events is the Events Field in the middle of the park.

The buildings, which are being restored, form a counterpoint to the greenery of the park. The finest of them date from the early days of the gasworks and were designed by the master builder Isaac Gosschalk. Others are less striking for their architectural beauty – although the cast-ironwork in the interior of the Gasholder is unique – but equally form part of an industrial heritage which makes the Westergasfabriek special.

The Westergasfabriek will soon again be one of the focal points of cultural activities in Amsterdam, as it was in the nineties. After restoration, the former industrial structures will accommodate many different cultural companies and organizations. Some of these will find a permanent place in one of the buildings, while others will rent space for specific events in the shorter term. Of those spaces, the largest is the Gasholder with a floor area of 3,000 square metres. It has already proved an excellent location for all sorts of activities in recent years.

Besides the park, the buildings and the cultural designation, the Westergasfabriek concept comprises elements that are not immediately obvious. There are few visible traces of the most costly part of the project: cleaning up the heavily polluted soil left behind by the gasworks during its decades of operation.

To go along with the new Westergasfabriek, there are new forms of 'cultural entrepreneurship'. The former gasworks already demonstrated its attractiveness as a venue during the last ten years under the banner of what was called the Interim Use. Necessarily, many of the activities that took place enjoyed little or no public subsidy. This forced the users to take a relatively pragmatic, independent attitude, which proved to foster greater freedom and dynamism. Another aspect of cultural entrepreneurship is that it is not the government that

is adapting the buildings to their new function, but a private property developer. New relations between culture and the market are thus manifested at various levels in the Westergasfabriek project.

Despite their diversity, the elements that make up the Westergasfabriek concept are not unconnected. On the contrary, they intersect in countless ways. The park, the cultural activities and the cultural entrepreneurship that generates those activities will all contribute to a unique atmosphere in the Westergasfabriek. Continual integration was necessary in the process that led up to the new Westergasfabriek. For example, the park design had to allow for the measures needed to deal with the soil pollution, and conversely the choice of environmental measures took the park design into account. Now the buildings are being dealt with too. The original intention was for the cultural activities to proceed uninterrupted throughout the operation, but this was eventually prevented by setbacks in the soil cleanup project.

Interior of the Gasholder

Nordsternpark, Gelsenkirchen (Germany).
The Bundesgartenschau (horticultural show) took place here in 1997.

A number of mechanical diggers were brought together in a disused lignite mine in the vicinity of Bitterfeld (then East Germany). Together they form Ferropolis, an extraordinary venue for large open-air concerts.

IBA Emscher Park
(Landschaftspark Duisburg-
Nord), Germany.
The Thyssen steel company
installed a blast furnace here in
1903. It remained in production
until 1985. In 1989, work started
on laying out a park to a design
by the landscape architect Peter
Latz. Many of the impressive
structures were preserved. The
buildings are used for cultural
activities.

So there was not just a single process, but a number of processes that often interacted, despite each having its own timescale and momentum. The integration of these processes was so essential that it became part of the concept in its own right.

The special combination of plans and processes makes the Westergasfabriek redevelopment a unique project. Still, there are noteworthy points of resemblance to comparable operations in the Netherlands and abroad. More and more cities in the industrialized world are finding themselves faced with tasks not unlike that of the Westergasfabriek. Countless urban locations – many of them indeed in inner city zones – contain redundant factory sites, marshalling yards, docks etc. awaiting new functions. There are common ingredients we can usually identify in the most successful of these brownfield redevelopments.

A major source of inspiration for the Westergasfabriek was *Internationale Bauausstellung (IBA) Emscher Park*, the international building exhibition held in the northern part of the Ruhr, Germany, from 1989 to 1999. Faced with the task of arousing enthusiasm for the Westergasfabriek redevelopment, it will come as no surprise that the project planners scheduled several trips to Emscher Park. At first sight there is admittedly little resemblance between the projects. The Westergasfabriek occupies an area of barely fifteen hectares, whereas IBA Emscher Park is spread over a region measuring eighty by thirty kilometres, with over two million inhabitants, along the valley of the small River Emscher. The total investment for IBA Emscher Park was some two thousand million Euros. Nonetheless there are striking parallels in the starting points, the approaches and the objectives between the two projects.

IBA Emscher Park was an initiative of the Federal State of Nordrhein-Westfalen. With their purposeful spatial strategy, they aimed to breathe new life into this part of the Ruhr, which had been struggling for years owing to the severe decline of mining and heavy industry. For this purpose, the Federal State deployed the tried and tested model of the *Internationale Bauausstellung,* a device used several times in Germany during the last eighty years to give a new impetus to building and design. The first IBA had resulted in the famous Weißenhofsiedlung in Stuttgart, where an elite corps of modern architects gave a stunning demonstration of the possibilities of 1920s modern architecture.

In the case of Emscher Park, the IBA was as much about planning strategies as about concrete designs. The dozens of individual projects fell in several different categories, and included the construction of three thousand dwellings, a landscape project to restore the natural course of the River Emscher and link fragmented areas of greenery, new technology centres, job creation projects and rehabilitation of the *Industriekultur* (a term referring to the collection of industrial heritage objects unmatched in quality and quantity). All these endeavours were intended to revive the fortunes of a region in the grip of a combined environmental and socioeconomic decline.

The task of most interest from the viewpoint of the Westergasfabriek was that of giving new uses to the industrial heritage. IBA Emscher Park illustrates how former industrial and mining complexes can exert an irresistible appeal, which can be consciously deployed to make places and regions more attractive. The best proof of this is *Landschaftspark Duisburg-Nord*, a 200 hectare site which contained a steelworks until 1985. Here, a large proportion of the buildings and equipment were left standing. Under the umbrella of the IBA, the whole site was transformed into a park in which the array of buildings, ruins and dismantled machinery now forms an attractive ensemble. The renovated buildings house amenities like restaurants and a theatre. A water-filled gasholder provides a facility for divers to practise their skills, and rock climbers can hone their technique on lofty old walls. The dismantled machinery, several pieces of which tower above the site, has no function but to impress the eye; and some of these structures are open to visitors, who can climb the stairs to enjoy a magnificent view of the park and the city. The 117.5 metre-tall gasholder in Oberhausen, the Zollverein XII complex in Essen and the Jahrhunderthalle in Bochum all exert a similar enchantment. Remains that people used to think of as merely getting in the way have turned into structures that impart a sense of pride and dignity to the former mining and industrial district.

In other respects, too, the Westergasfabriek project has benefited from the experience of IBA Emscher Park. The IBA organizers concentrated strongly on the development process and its strategies – as did those of the Westergasfabriek project. The IBA moreover demonstrated that the focus must lie on the integration of various processes and on achieving good communications among all those involved, particularly including the residents.

Lessons could also be drawn from aspects that went less smoothly. For example, the IBA neglected the programming of its projects. Too much attention was trained on the hardware, on designing the public space and renovating the buildings. It was sometimes forgotten that, to bring a place to life, you also need software – that the public space and buildings need activities to attract the public. Another problem is that management of the heritage objects of IBA Emscher Park is rather decentralized, with the result that valuable insights and experience could go to waste through fragmentation.

Another source of inspiration, and one which differs considerably from IBA Emscher Park, has been the restructuring of the defunct docks and industry zone of the Spanish city of Bilbao. Over three hundred million Euros have been invested in this project since it started, under the name of *Bilbao Ría 2000*, in 1992. Like the IBA, it is thus on a scale that bears little resemblance to that of Westergasfabriek, but in strategic respects there are definite similarities.

The Jahrhunderthalle, Bochum (Germany), was thoroughly restored in the 1990s but then remained unused. After further alterations, the hall is now the main venue for the Ruhr Triennial, a large-scale arts festival directed by Gerard Mortier.

The master plan by Cesar Pelli, showing the Abandoibarra docks in Bilbao redeveloped as the new city centre.

Bilbao was until recent decades a city whose river banks were dominated by docks and associated heavy industry. These activities had long been a source of prosperity, but by the late eighties they had largely vanished. Industry collapsed and unemployment had soared to thirty percent. The apparent hopelessness of the situation also sapped the city's morale.

It was a time that cried out for someone to emerge – someone who could convince everyone that the only way was up, and that the city would have to pull itself out of the mire by its own bootstraps. Not forgetting the city alderman who instigated the redevelopment, the main individual who galvanized the city into action was Pablo Otaola, who remained the driving force behind Bilbao Ría 2000 until recently. It is mainly thanks to these two that Bilbao Ría 2000 became a hugely ambitious operation to transform a rundown industrial city into an attractive centre for service enterprises and culture. The space needed for redevelopment was available in the abandoned docks and industry zones.

Like IBA Emscher Park, Bilbao Ría 2000 set itself a series of goals. A prominent feature of the plans was a major investment in infrastructure. New roads and bridges were built to reestablish the relation between the city and the river. Another addition was a splendid new metro system, whose stations are nicknamed *Fosteritos* after their designer Norman Foster. But it is the cultural initiatives that have really placed Bilbao in the limelight of international interest. These include a new centre for the performing arts and – as the undisputed icon of the new Bilbao – the Guggenheim Museum designed by Frank Gehry.

The visible results of Bilbao Ría 2000 (particularly those in the cultural sector) are not all that have inspired similar projects elsewhere. People were impressed by the way the process was organized – even more than in the case of IBA Emscher Park. To start with, Otaola worked by preference with a small team of highly motivated individuals. The project leadership could not rely on

Bilbao's dockland activities made way for elegantly appointed public space and the Guggenheim Museum

extensive powers to obtain results; such powers were limited, as they were for the IBA and the Westergasfabriek. At the regular meetings, Otaola was forced to argue his case before a number, sometimes dozens, of participants, including the financing authorities (half the shares are owned by the State and the rest by local government) and public/private organizations. It is to Otaola's credit that he succeeded in cultivating a spirit of cooperation among this heterogeneous group of individuals and organizations (the Basque parties are dominant in the region and the city). Bilbao, Emscher Park and the Westergasfabriek all show that steering such enterprises relies more on communicative skills and persuasiveness than on holding a position of authority.

Bilbao illustrates better than anywhere that a galvanizing vision is the first requirement for success in transforming brownfield areas, and that the vision must then be propagated in a vigorous and appealing way. Words alone are not enough: fragments of the new future must be made visible as soon as possible. This concretization can take different forms, ranging from the Interim Use of the Westergasfabriek to the Guggenheim Museum in Bilbao.

It would seem that the new function, often a cultural one, given to disused industrial heritage sites reflects changes that are affecting cities all over the Western world. It is not insignificant that these changes have their main impact on those cities that epitomize the explosive growth of industrialization of the nineteenth and early twentieth centuries. Factories, railway yards and docks were built at what were then the city margins. Almost invariably, these locations had strategic value, not too far from the city centre and with good access by road, water and rail.

During the latter part of the twentieth century, a gradual metamorphosis towards the post-industrial city began. The city became less dependent on industry, and hence the physical connection between the historical city and its industrial or industry-related activities weakened. Since the built up area had

meanwhile sprawled far and wide, new industrial sites were located farther and farther from the historic centre. Freight transport also disappeared from the city scene, with marshalling yards and distribution centres being abandoned one by one. Rotterdam may be the world's biggest port, but little of this is evident in the city itself – the ships dock at Europort, twenty to thirty kilometres to the west. Many labour-intensive industries have indeed vanished altogether. Shipbuilding, mining and textiles have moved en masse to low-wage countries. Gas generation, finally, was one of those industries that simply became obsolete.

The cities thus lost some of their physical *raison d'être*. The latter was replaced by functions and activities that were less strongly tied to a particular locality. An insurance company or TV studio has more freedom of choice in where to set up business than a coal mine or car plant. The cities became interwoven, moreover, with less tangible, virtual structures. The obvious example is of course the growth of electronic information networks. Communications technology has made it unnecessary for all share trading to go on in the same building, and the Dutch electronics giant Philips was able to move its headquarters from Eindhoven, where the factories are, to the financial and cultural centre of the Netherlands, Amsterdam.

It is not only in the respect of information and communications technology that the concrete city is loaded with the software of activities that are less material in character, for this also applies to sectors such as the media, services, education and culture. The less cities can fall back on the certainties of their original industrial rationale, the more they have to invest in sectors like these. They are not only important for the jobs they generate, but also because they show up the city as an attractive place to live in, work in or visit.

Meanwhile, the traditional spatial concept of the city, with a centre, suburbs, a periphery and surrounding countryside, is due for revision. The original centre is no longer automatically the place that exerts the greatest pull. The city has become part of a force field in which many other attractors are operative. The main terminal of the new high-speed rail line in the Netherlands will not be Amsterdam's Central Station, but *Amsterdam Zuid* (South) in the Zuidas development zone, which is already becoming a favoured location for multinational company headquarters.

A parallel development is that by which many cities decreasingly function as autonomous units; particularly in densely populated areas, the cities are tending to merge into larger networks in which they form a coherent entity with others. In a 'network city' of this kind, places that used to be considered peripheral become new centres of development. That defunct industrial areas can suddenly find themselves in this position is illustrated by the London docklands, Kop van Zuid in Rotterdam and Bilbao as mentioned above. The Westergasfabriek, too, profits not only from its convenient location near the inner city but also from its vicinity to Sloterdijk, a palpable decentral network node where transport lines intersect.

Just as the background of a site like the Westergasfabriek represents the city's industrial past, its newly designated use proclaims the city's future. The transformations of these brownfield sites are exemplary of the radical change processes, both visible and invisible, that affect the city. The grimy factory smoke is replaced by the 'clean' image of greenery and culture. Locations where products used to be manufactured, goods loaded or coal extracted, are now turned to advantage to make the city more appealing. This puts them in a better position to compete with other cities whose original, material rationale is similarly under threat.

There are further similarities to be observed between the successful projects, in the benefits obtained from converting their brownfield sites. In most cases the projects result in an enhanced quality of public space. The areas concerned are usually substandard, for example with low-value housing crowded along narrow streets with little if any greenery.

Creating a new park in one of these areas can be a significant improvement. A number of good examples may be seen in Paris. On the former Citroën factory grounds along the Seine, the *Parc André Citroën* has been created; the site of the present *Parc de la Villette* contained slaughterhouses until 1974; and the *Parc de Bercy* used to be an area with long rows of wine warehouses. IBA Emscher Park, too, placed a priority on the creation of green, parkland areas.

Former docks and industrial zones can similarly be developed into good locations for companies that buttress the city's economic basis. London's Docklands are already vying with the City as a preferred location for large financial institutions.

Companies and institutions operating in the field of culture and the media are also growing increasingly significant in the dynamic of the contemporary city. Old industrial buildings can be a practically and aesthetically suitable

Parc André Citroën, Paris

Docklands, London

environment for them, as became clear during the Interim Use phase of the Westergasfabriek. This is also illustrated by the former mining complex *Zollverein XII* in Essen, Germany, where a number of leading design companies are moving into the Bauhaus-inspired buildings (part of IBA Emscher Park) around the *Design Zentrum* fitted out by Norman Foster.

In parallel with the creation of an attractive public space, culture is the main new designated use of these sites. This is particularly evident where the original buildings survive in whole or in part. Industrial heritage buildings provide excellent locations for art galleries, theatres and other cultural applications. They often have large, empty, robust interiors that can be utilized in a wide variety of ways.

Besides their practical flexibility, it is the distinctive atmosphere of these buildings that makes them so well suited to cultural applications. Sometimes, as in the case of the Westergasfabriek, the architecture is of a high standard. But even for those buildings that are architecturally less noteworthy, their robustness, their state of decay halted but tangible enough to arouse romantic sentiments, and the collective memory of the industrial history they embody, all contribute to their great charm. Nowadays, especially, it is these unsentimental, 'imperfect' surroundings that do most justice to cultural events.

Numerous examples can also be cited of industrial buildings and complexes that have subsequently been accorded a cultural use. In the Netherlands, besides the Westergasfabriek, these include *De Witte Dame* ('The White Lady') in Eindhoven, a former Philips factory which now houses a centre for design and culture. In Tilburg, the De Pont museum for contemporary art is housed in an old wool mill. Other countries also have placed museums for modern art in redundant factories and mine buildings, for example the Musée des Arts Contemporains in Le Grand-Hornu (near Mons, Belgium), MASS MoCA in North Adams (Massachusetts, US) and – not to be forgotten – the highly

Le Grand-Hornu, Hornu, Belgium

MASS MoCA,
North Adams, Massachusetts

successful Tate Modern in London, which occupies the immense hall of a former power station beside the Thames. IBA Emscher Park, too, yielded a theatre in one of the buildings in Landschaftspark Duisburg-Nord, and the Jahrhunderthalle in Bochum, a famous factory hall, over a century old, which has been adapted to house large stage productions and concerts.

Designating industrial heritage buildings for cultural uses is consistent with the profound changes the cities are undergoing. Culture has always had a strong connection with cities, but nowadays the arts are being deployed in every conceivable guise to give the city its 'identity'. The most striking illustration of this is again Bilbao, where Frank Gehry's Guggenheim Museum transformed the city almost instantly into a major public attraction. As many cities have discovered, Bilbao realized there was no better way of standing out from its competitors than by embracing culture. By putting the arts in a setting where the city of the past, the city of heavy industry and physical labour, is tangible all around, the metamorphosis of the city is almost literally depicted.

De Pont, Tilburg, Netherlands

Through its transformation into a city park plus a contemporary centre for cultural activities, the Westergasfabriek is thus one of a family of similar projects for restructuring and redesigning brownfield sites, disregarding the considerable differences in scale and context. The intense interest the Westergasfabriek has attracted from both at home and abroad has marked it out as a trend-setter. Project manager Evert Verhagen is regularly invited to speak about the Westergasfabriek concept at international conferences on brownfield site development. In 1998, the Westergasfabriek was indeed exhaustively documented in an international study by the US Environmental Protection Agency (EPA). The EPA report concludes that the strategy applied in the Westergasfabriek project – in particular, the combination of temporary utiliza-

Tate Modern, Londen

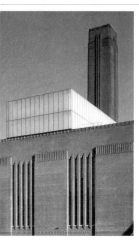

tion with simultaneous planning for a definitively designated use – is a paradigm for towns faced with the reutilization of polluted sites.

The EPA report also notes how important an open-ended, comprehensive planning process has been to the success of the Westergasfabriek project. That, too, was part of the concept. Like projects elsewhere, the Westergasfabriek has shown that a flexible and decisive project organization is vital to success. I will return to the importance of a well designed process later.

The same is true for other elements of the concept: the 'hardware' of the new park, the buildings and the soil cleanup, and the 'software' of the cultural functions. In the latter, the intention is to make the Westergasfabriek into a laboratory of cultural entrepreneurship, which can explore both the opportunities and the limitations of relations between culture and the market.

When the Westergasfabriek buildings were made available for cultural activities in early 1993 – initially for one year only – it had already been over 25 years since gas was last generated there. Even before the vast underground reservoir of natural gas was discovered in the northern Netherlands, the production of coal gas had been taken over by the Hoogovens works in IJmuiden, and the Westergasfabriek was used only for producing water gas. Gas production finally ceased altogether on 28 March 1967. The Municipal Energy Company (GEB) continued to use the site for purposes such as workshops and equipment storage.

1882 – The Westergasfabriek was built between the Haarlemmervaart canal and the bend in the railway.

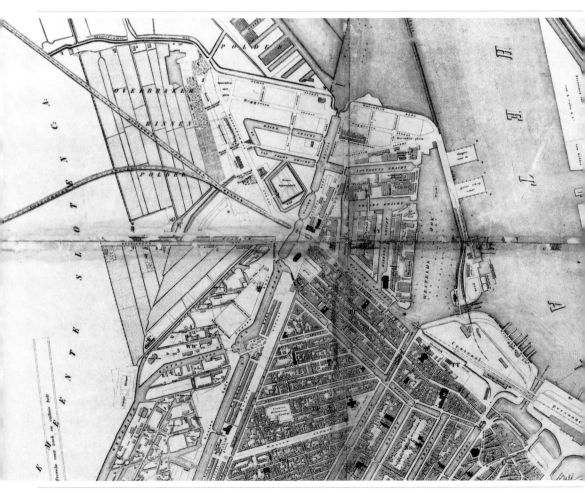

interim use

The coal heaps disappeared, and with them the characteristic smell associated with gas production. The remarkable architecture of the old factory buildings was not recognized until some of them – including a splendid retort house – had already been demolished. It was not until years later the surviving buildings were listed for protection as historic monuments.

The Westergasfabriek operated as a functioning gasworks for a total of around eighty years. Barely two years after the city council had granted a concession to the London-based Imperial Continental Gas Association (ICGA) in

Westergasfabriek water tower, 1903

1883, a complete gas manufacturing plant stood in place and was ready to distribute coal gas to the city.

The unprecedented beauty of these buildings, especially for an industrial complex, was the achievement of Isaac Gosschalk. This architect, born in 1837, was a leading representative of the *Hollandse Neorenaissance*, an architectural style in vogue in the Netherlands at the end of the nineteenth century. Together with Groningen railway station, the Westergasfabriek is among the most important works of Gosschalk's oeuvre.

The architecture of the Westergasfabriek was elegantly described in a booklet produced by the municipal historic buildings department in 1998 on commission of the Westergasfabriek project team: *Westergasfabriek, het terrein en de gebouwen* (Westergasfabriek, the Grounds and Buildings; Bureau Monumentenzorg). The booklet states that the Westergasfabriek has all the hallmarks of the neo-Renaissance, although the eclectic Gosschalk did not hesitate to incorporate other stylistic elements here and there. The result was a wealth of form, most of which harks back to the Dutch Renaissance architecture of the sixteenth and seventeenth centuries. Gosschalk's favourite material was red and yellow brick, but he also used a certain amount of natural stone. 'Neoclassicist' stucco was something he detested. Gosschalk's historicist style did not debar him from using innovative structural methods. We encounter one of the finest instances of these under the roof of the purifier building, with characteristic Polonceau trusses; the advantages of this construction method lie in its lower material requirement and the higher free space under the span structure.

The largest buildings on the site, which were completed in 1885, were the purifier building and the retort house. The latter was demolished in 1961 after the production of coal gas was taken over by Hoogovens in IJmuiden. Between the purifier building and the retort house there stood a series of smaller build-

The gas manufacturing process: retort, condensers, purifier boxes and gasholder

Purifier Building, interior

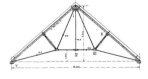

Polonceau truss: two trussed beams with a tie bar and an additional hanger rod in the middle

Retort House

ings, among them the machine building, two metering stations and a water tower. The beauty of the last of these failed to save it from demolition in 1968. Other buildings that Gosschalk designed on the site were an ammonia plant (demolished in 1933), two supervisor's houses, the regulator house (where the gas pressure was controlled), 'boilerhouse 9', an engineer's house and the large workshop building, which has been the seat of the urban district council since the late nineteen eighties.

The city of Amsterdam took over the gasworks from ICGA in 1898, after which the complex was enlarged. For example, a boilerhouse was added next to the ammonia plant at the western extremity of the site in 1901. A year after that, building work began on 'the biggest gasholder on the European continent', behind the three existing smaller gasholders adjacent to the Haarlemmervaart canal. The structure now known as the Gasholder is actually the round substruc-

Transportation of coal

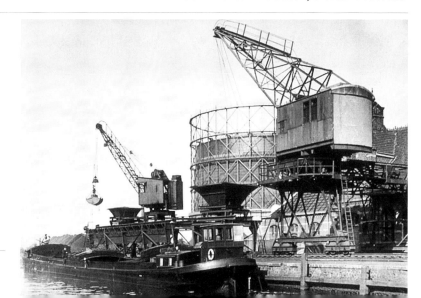

A. Klönne, Dortmund.
Amsterdam 16. IX. 02.

Construction of the large
Gasholder in 1902

ture on which the gasholder proper once stood. The huge columnless hall of this substructure, with a diameter of sixty metres, was formerly used as a storage facility. The boilerhouse adjacent to the machine building was completed in 1903, followed by a boilerhouse-cum-laboratory (later known as the Ladderhouse) in 1904, and, in 1905, a regulator house and a water gas plant, the last of which was converted into a transformer station in 1966.

In the fifty years after the building flurry of the early nineteen hundreds, only a few smaller buildings were added. Curiously, some further substantial investments were made right near the end of the gasworks' existence, as though the Westergasfabriek were trying to give one final, noisy kick of life. In 1955, a new gasholder came into operation, and a new water gas plant was built on the foundations of part of the old retort house. Shortly afterwards, when production had been halted, the latter plant was converted into a laboratory. Its architectural value was limited, and it was the only large building to be demol-

Westergasfabriek, approx. 1935

ished to make room for the new park in the late nineties. In 1962, finally, another new gasholder was commissioned. Presumably nobody realized at that point in time that production of natural gas was to begin in less than a year, making the gasworks redundant. After a brief period of service, both gasholders were dismantled in 1974.

With gas production at an end, various prospective uses emerged for the well-situated site. Among them were plans to erect a tram depot, to build a train washing yard and to widen Haarlemmerweg into a four-lane arterial road – a development that would have meant the end of much of the original Westerpark.

It was the last scheme, in particular, that aroused resistance among local residents; for it was in the period, around 1970, when neighbourhood activism was rampant. The activism later diminished, but the residents' organizations kept up the fight to have the Westergasfabriek designated for 'green' functions. They had historic documents to back them up on this: a map from 1875, even before the gasworks existed, showed the city had already designated the site (which lay partly over the border in the adjacent municipality of Sloten) to become part of a much enlarged Westerpark.

The Amsterdam council proved susceptible to the residents' arguments. After the latter occupied a nearby farm in protest against degradation of the polder landscape by the construction of a new railway, the council appointed a working committee of officials in late 1978. Their task was to prepare the Overbrakerpolder – a landscape that included Westerpark and the Westergasfabriek – for a new, green designation. The resulting land use ordinance, which was passed by the city council in 1981, assigned a recreational function to the Westergasfabriek.

In 1984, an expanded Westerpark briefly entered the picture as a potential location for the 1992 Floriade horticultural exhibition. The honour eventually went to Zoetermeer, however, for among other reasons because the organizers feared excessive delays due to the contaminated soil. Instead, a preliminary design appeared in 1985 in which the Westerpark was to be expanded in the same 'English' landscape style as the existing park.

In the years that followed, it was again the soil contamination that stood in the way of speedy implementation of the plans. A decontamination study would first be required to establish the nature and extent of the pollution, and to elaborate a number of variants for the cleanup procedure. The most feasible (that is, the cheapest) solution emerged in the study of what was termed the isolation variant. This meant, instead of cleaning up or removing the contaminated soil, 'packaging' it by encircling it with a dam of sheetpiling and covering it with asphalt. Not only would this solution have prevented expansion of the park, but it had a further major drawback. The Ministry of Housing, Spatial Planning and the Environment, which was to provide most of the funding, insist-

Construction of fourth gasholder, 1953

Gasholder in use as storage facility of the Municipal Energy Company, mid 1960s

ed that the area retain the same designated use as before the cleanup: in the present case, a parking and storage facility.

For the residents' groups, who had joined forces to form *Westerpark-overleg* (the 'Westerpark Consultative Committee'), this outcome was unacceptable. This committee called in an environmental consultant of its own, and this consultant proposed the 'isolation plus' variant. In this, the polluted soil would be sealed off as in the 'isolation' variant, but the top layer would now consist of clean soil instead of asphalt. This would make it possible to have a park after all. Since the park design of 1985, which included a lake, would no be longer possible under the isolation plus variant, the joint residents' groups approached a design agency to prepare a new outline scheme.

Meanwhile, another delaying factor reared its head. In the late eighties, Amsterdam began decentralizing its municipal organization. Most of the city was divided up into a number of urban districts, each with its own elected council. One of these councils was the urban district of Westerpark, which, on its foundation in 1990, inherited the Westergasfabriek project from the 'central city', as the original city authority was called after decentralization. Coordination and implementation of the project remained at first the responsibility the central city, but a year later, the obligation to do business with the city ceased, and the district took on the coordination for itself.

Although the transfer of the project to the urban district was later to prove advantageous in many respects, at first it made the situation of the Westergasfabriek if anything more difficult. For a start, the responsibilities and financial consequences of the transfer inevitably took time and effort to arrange. The transfer process itself was chaotic. City agencies such as the Environment Department which were closely involved with the Westergasfabriek had to get used to the new relations of authority, and the urban district had itself yet to find its feet. Besides, nobody had any experience with complicated projects like the Westergasfabriek.

Making his debut along with the urban district was Evert Verhagen, a man who was rapidly to become the chief initiator behind the Westergasfabriek project, as well as its public face. Verhagen, who had already proved his considerable organizational capability in Amsterdam-Zuidoost, was initially appointed by the urban district as 'sector head in charge of district works'. Although he took an intense interest in the Westergasfabriek project from the outset, it was initially just one aspect of his duties among several. A project manager was appointed to run the actual project. However, when the appointed manager fell out of line with the open-ended, non-linear planning process Verhagen had in mind (about which more will be said in Chapter 5), Verhagen decided to take over the project management task and occupy himself full time with the Westergasfabriek.

The residents' organizations viewed the new urban district with suspicion. They saw the decentralization process, in which the district councils were put forward as official representatives of the residents, as a political attempt to seize control of democracy at a local level. The more activistic neighbourhood organizations feared that the urban district would try to undermine their legitimacy as spokespersons of the residents.

A first obstacle thus loomed up in relations between the newly founded urban district and the neighbourhood organizations. As a preamble to the final choice of a park architect, the district decided to invite a number of design firms to prepare an outline design. In retrospect, this was an ill-judged manoeuvre in which the district effectively snubbed the Westerparkoverleg; after all, the latter had only just had a structure sketch prepared under its own steam. The issue was resolved by appointing an independent consultant who was to prepare for the selection of a park architect by formulating a schedule of requirements. The choice of design firm made by the neighbourhood organizations would not be ignored in this process.

Early in 1991, Hans Warnau was invited to apply for the function of independent consultant. Warnau, who died in 1995, was one of the most respected landscape architects in the Netherlands. He drew up a schedule of requirements for the Westergasfabriek, but it stayed locked in a drawer for several years because of the lack of headway on the question of soil decontamination. The urban district and the Ministry of Housing, Spatial Planning and the Environment reached a stalemate on this issue in 1992. Taking the isolation-plus variant for which the municipality had opted meant, according to the ministry, that any soil moved from one place to another on the site would first have to be decontaminated. This implied roughly a doubling of the costs.

If today we compare the schedule drawn up by Warnau with the design by Kathryn Gustafson, the points of similarity are striking. He had already foreseen both the position of the Events Field and the slope behind it.

In late 1991, the grounds and buildings of the Westergasfabriek were still in use by the municipal energy company. Their departure was now once again post-poned, but the district council thought the time was ripe for deciding a new designated use for the buildings. An 'appeal for ideas' was launched, in which individuals and organizations were invited to submit their plans. Several months later, a committee led by the architect Herman Zeinstra found itself faced with a mountain of no less than 334 entries to judge. A jury was also appointed to hand out a number of monetary prizes for the most original and inspiring submissions, regardless of their feasibility.

The adjudication committee recommended the urban district to commis-sion three entries and one combination of entries to be worked out in further detail. The district council adopted this recommendation and decided in June 1992 to authorize four feasibility studies. This resulted six months later in four concrete plans: a Museum of Civil Engineering, an Amsterdam Centre for the Arts, a centre for modern music and a plan called the 'Rhizome Scenario'. The first two quickly fell by the wayside, leaving the decision to be fought out between the music centre and the Rhizome plan.

The Centre for Modern Music was an idea of Jan Wolff, director of *De IJsbreker* contemporary music centre. Wolff intended De IJsbreker to join forces at the Westergasfabriek with related organizations such as Donemus and Gaudeamus; his initiative therefore subsequently went under the name of the 'IJsbreker Coalition'.

The Rhizome Scenario came from Chris de Vries – a local resident, the ex-chairman of the Spaarndammerbuurt Neighbourhood Centre and a cofounder of the Polanen Theatre. De Vries took the name of his proposal from the work of Gilles Deleuze. This French philosopher, popular at the time, used the metaphor of branching underground plants (rhizomes) as a way of describ-ing subjective, hierarchy-free structures. The Rhizome plan involved making the buildings available for diverse and to some extent spontaneous uses by local residents and organizations.

It came as no surprise when the neighbourhood centres in Spaarndammerbuurt and Staatsliedenbuurt put their weight behind De Vries's plan. The urban district council nonetheless opted for the music centre, on a proposal of the district alderman responsible for the Westergasfabriek, Hansen, because the scheme looked financially more feasible. All the same, the Rhizome plan was not completely ditched despite being thought insufficiently profitable. The district council invited Chris de Vries to advise on utilization of the buildings that were not to become part of the music centre. However, the residents' organizations found it difficult to reconcile themselves to the inferior status of 'their' plan. Considering the battle they had been waging for years, they understandably saw the Westergasfabriek as an amenity for their own dis-trict, whereas the plan of the IJsbreker Coalition was for a *national* centre of modern music.

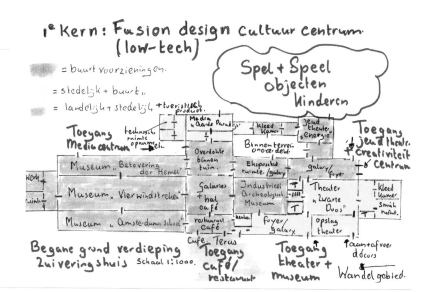

A page from the Rhizome Plan by
Chris de Vries

Rhapsody in Green, a plan
submitted in response to the
appeal for ideas

By the latter half of 1992, the period of the above-mentioned feasibility studies, the time arrived when the energy corporation would at last leave the Westergasfabriek. Assuming the buildings were emptied out in the course of 1993, it was bound to take at least another year before they could be spruced up and modified for their officially defined functions. The urban district felt little inclination to leave the Westergasfabriek unused in the meanwhile. Various interested parties, among them the Holland Festival, had already enquired whether the gasworks could be made available for holding arts and entertainment events. Verhagen decided to organize the temporary utilization of the buildings on a broader footing, and in the autumn of 1992 he appointed Liesbeth Jansen as a 'project leader for events'. Jansen, who had worked for the Mickery Theatre, had many contacts in Amsterdam cultural circles. Since Verhagen took responsibility for most of the practical questions such as finance, as well as for negotiations with the urban district,

Jansen had the space to devote her attention entirely to her cultural duties.

The *Interim Use*, as it was called, was to take effect on 1 May 1993. Jansen could thus assume she had six months to prepare everything. But she had hardly set to work when she discovered how little could be taken for granted about the Westergasfabriek. No sooner was she installed in her little office in the Regulator House than the news arrived that the city energy corporation planned to abandon most of the complex in less than two weeks time. It was considered unwise to leave the buildings empty for six months, for there was a real likelihood that they would fall prey to squatters, and the urban district would then have little control over their future utilization. So the six months of preparation time quickly proved to be wishful thinking, and Jansen immediately had to set about finding temporary users. Public events, however, could still not take place until 1 June 1993, by which time the energy corporation would have completely withdrawn from the site and

Liesbeth Jansen,
Interim Use project leader

the urban district would have taken full responsibility for its security.

Little effort was required to kindle interest in the buildings. Most candidate users presented themselves of their own accord, and agreements were quickly settled with the first tenants. Among them were Studio Wenck, who were in search of a film studio after being forced to abandon their former premises in Wenckenbachweg, and Patchwork, an artists' collective whose activities at the Westergasfabriek were to include making the huge, floating, paraffin-wax soaked ball gowns that they then launched on the Hofvijver, the lake of the Dutch Houses of Parliament in the Hague.

Although there was no time for a calmly considered approach, Jansen was loth to rent the buildings on a first come first served basis. Had she done so, the site would have quickly filled up with the stream of artists who regularly approached her in search of studios; but that was not what she had in mind. Without an opportunity to programme the Interim Use from the ground up,

Westergasfabriek grounds in the 1980s

Kantine West

West Pacific, pavement café

Jansen decided it ought at least be exciting and varied. That was indeed her main selection criterion: not too much 'more of the same', and prospective tenants would have to bring the ingredients for a surprising cultural life along with them. It also meant that users could not be indifferent to the buildings and the location. A strong affinity with the place was essential to the rapid creation of a distinctive atmosphere.

The word quickly went around cultural Amsterdam that space would soon be available, with the result that most prospective tenants appeared spontaneously. There was one particular amenity that Jansen considered vital to the cultural dynamic, and which she actively sought: a bar or restaurant that would be a meeting place for users and visitors. In those otherwise still desolate surroundings, an enterprise of that kind would be the germ from which the venue could flourish.

In her search, she came across someone who had made 'temporary catering establishments' his business. Koen Vollaers had for years accompanied travelling theatre festivals such as the renowned *Boulevard of Broken Dreams* with his transportable restaurant *Cantina Mobilé*. Vollaers was a hospitality specialist with the talent and physical resources to transform the abandoned industrial canteen at one end of the Purifier Building quickly into a restaurant with a distinct atmosphere. The industrial ambiance of Formica tables and plastic tablecloths (not to mention a kitchen of serious substance) merited a prosaic-sounding name: *Kantine West*.

Kantine West immediately lived up to expectations. Exactly as intended, it became the place where everyone who felt kinship with the Westergasfabriek gathered. Once it became clear, moreover, that the Interim Use was not going to be limited to just one year, the restaurant began to gain a momentum of its own. It occurred to Vollaers, for example, to open out the vehicles of his mobile restaurant, parked for the winter in an adjoining space, and to position one of his trailers as a stage. With a minimum of new investment he thus established the basis for *Club de Ville*, a dance venue that was to flourish for years as an alternative for those who felt the usual house parties were too massive, too frenzied and too commercial.

The restaurant, originally intended to survive for one season only, is one of the few components of the Interim Use period to remain in existence to this day. Since autumn 2002, it has returned to its original form and is now once more called Kantine West after having been dubbed *West Pacific* for most of the intervening period. The latter name was adopted when the restaurant was transformed into a bar-cum-restaurant using an interior originating from the former Pacific Café in Rotterdam. The Pacific, which had just shut down, was owned by the parents of disc jockey Lex Breet, whom Vollaers knew from his Boulevard period. It was not long before Breet and the estimable chef Koen van Brunschot became Vollaers' partners in West Pacific. While Van Brunschot brought West Pacific up to scratch in the culinary department, Breet took charge of the musical side of an original formula: daily, at eleven PM, the tables would be pushed aside so that the dinner guests could prolong their evening's entertainment with dancing.

Six months after the first tenants settled into the Westergasfabriek, the public were allowed in too. The first performance in the Gasholder, the opera Antigone by Ton de Leeuw, immediately became the high point of the 1993 Holland Festival. Antigone highlighted the spectacular possibilities of the huge structure. After expulsion of the hundreds of pigeons who inhabited the round space, trucks full of the sand, timber and scaffolding needed to furnish the interior started rumbling in and out of the space. Many more opera performances were to take place in the years that followed in the Gasholder, whose capacity for an audience of 2,000 people made it the largest opera hall in the Netherlands.

'En Aria' opera in the Purifier Building

Performance of Discordia in the
Transformer Building

Il Florilegio, circus

Pietje, opera

Winterparade in the Gasholder

Club de Ville discotheque, 1997

Fun fair at Westergasfabriek

Brazilian Carnival in the
Gasholder

Drum Rhythm Festival

Drum Rhythm Festival,
Yousour N'dour

Drum Rhythm Festival,
Trilok Gurtu

'Puck en Hans' fashion show in
the Purifier Building

Stockhausen's
Helicopter String Quartet

At the end of September 1993, it was announced that the Interim Use would be extended by a further year. 'Then the fun will be over,' wrote *Amsterdams Stadsblad*, still unaware that the temporary situation would endure for several years. The number of tenants gradually increased. Among them were *DasArts*, a postgraduate theatre school, *Household Hardware*, a wholesaler in Moroccan domestic articles, and the theatre company *Orkater*. Another theatre company, *Toneelgroep Amsterdam* (TGA), finally found in the Transformer House a chance to abandon the proscenium stage of the Stadsschouwburg (the civic theatre in the centre of Amsterdam) for the flat arena the group had so long sought under Gerardjan Reinders. Despite the temporary character of their tenancy, TGA did not hesitate to install a new floor and new wiring in the Transformer House, or to mount a logo in the form of a red lightning flash (conceived by the graphic designer Anthon Beeke) high on the outside wall. The Canadian circus *Cirque du Soleil* set up its European headquarters in the Laboratory Building (later demolished) among other things in the hope of establishing connections with Dutch cultural life.

While the long-term tenants ensured continuity, the short-term rental of buildings generated diversity and surprise. The Gasholder was used not only for operas but for fashion shows, exhibitions, new car launches, circuses and company banquets. Rocco Veenboer held his famous dance parties there – events, later called *Awakenings*, which developed over a number of years into veritable techno happenings. The buildings also provided backdrops for films, fashion shows, TV commercials and video clips (including one by the Chippendales).

From 1995 onwards, a more commercial market was also opened up for occasional lettings. It was a period when companies, particularly those working in marketing and communications, took to organizing their conferences and other meetings as 'experiences'. The Westergasfabriek, especially the Gasholder, was an ideal setting for these.

De Modefabriek

Antique and Trends Fair in
the Gasholder

The list of events that took place in the Westergasfabriek from 1993 onwards
seems endless. A high point was the production of Karlheinz Stockhausen's
Helicopter String Quartet on 26 June 1995. The German composer had written
this work for the Salzburger Festspiele, but it was never achieved a performance
there owing to protests by environmental groups. As part of the Holland Festival,
the world premiere of Stockhausen's piece took place at the Westergasfabriek.
The members of the Arditti Quartet were ensconced in four separate air-force
helicopters which hovered above the site. Below, in the Transformer House,
Stockhausen sat at a mixing console channelling the composite of string
quartet music and rotor noise transmitted down from the helicopters, to the
audience in the hall.

The Westergasfabriek also proved to be a splendid location for outdoor festivals, in which both the buildings and the surrounding grounds could be turned
to advantage. Most festivals returned annually to the Westergasfabriek until
prevented by the soil decontamination work. The avant-garde art festival *Triple
X* first took place there in 1994. It was followed next year by the *Drum Rhythm
Festival*, with swinging musical styles ranging from hip hop and dance to 'world
music'. A review in the *Volkskrant* described Drum Rhythm as 'the most enjoy-
able festival in the Netherlands', and as 'a change from the usual two-day bath
of beer and mud'. Terts Brinkhof held several *Winterparade* theatre events in
the Gasholder.

A noteworthy festival, which took place four times starting in 1997 and
which was outstandingly apt to the Westergasfabriek atmosphere, was
Kunstvlaai. It was conceived by Jos Houweling, director of the Sandberg insti-
tute, a postgraduate art foundation. After seeing the once-only art fair *Art
Amsterdam* at the Westergasfabriek, Houweling had the idea that it would be
a good thing if there were an alternative to the 'established' annual art fair

Moda Mas, fashion show in
the Purifier Building

Fun fair at Westergasfabriek

Il Florilegio circus, horseback act

AmsterDam Diner
in the Gasholder

Set of Allegria, 1997

KunstRAI. The local artists' initiatives of the Netherlands, rather than the leading galleries, would show at Houweling's fair. The official KunstRAI objected to
the name Houweling first thought of, *Niet de KunstRAI* ('Not the KunstRAI'), so
the eventual name chosen was *Kunstvlaai* (literally, 'Art Tart'). The first
Kunstvlaai took place in the Machine Building and attracted five thousand visitors. The next year, other halls and some of the external space were also used
and the number of visitors doubled. Most of the artists' initiatives set up instal-
lations, such as a party tent from which the sound of a lecture could be heard,
and a tour of the site with a blind guide.

Liesbeth Jansen and her bureau admittedly steered a course for the
Interim Use by selecting the tenants but rarely acted as programme makers in
their own right. There was one significant exception: the festival *24 uur van de
Westergasfabriek* (24 Hours of the Westergasfabriek). This festival was intended
as a lighthearted 'village feast' with the principle roles reserved for the regular
users of the buildings and for residents of the surrounding neighbourhoods.
The intention was for all the creative energy concentrated in and around the
Westergasfabriek to burst forth in one great conflagration. Even tenants who
were located on the Westergasfabriek site but rarely held public activities, such
as the theatre company Orkater, were to make a showing. The festivals started
on Saturday afternoon and ended 24 hours later with a neighbourhood break-
fast party. The two festivals that took place were both a considerable success,
and included among other things performances by Orkater in a circus tent, the
actor Arjen Ederveen making *poffertjes* (Dutch miniature pancakes) and an
opportunity for members of the public to project their holiday snaps at cinema-
screen scale in the Boilerhouse.

The 24-hour Westergasfabriek festival was meant to be an annual event,
but it came to a (provisional) end after the second occurrence. Since the consequences of the soil cleanup were much more drastic than anticipated, most

Artist's installation in
Park of the Future exhibition,
1999

47

AmsterDam Diner

Chapel in Machine Building,
artist's installation in
Triple X Festival

4 Hours at the Westergasfabriek

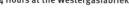

eft, Arjan Ederveen, 24 Hours at
he Westergasfabriek

public activities were temporarily halted in 2000. Although it was not the intention, these festivals can in retrospect be regarded as a fitting conclusion to the Interim Use, which began as a one-season affair but ended up lasting seven years.

The Interim Use was of course not immune to change in that period of seven years. At first, when nobody could have predicted it would last so long, the temporariness was uppermost in everyone's mind. Everything was new and spontaneous and, as Jansen said at the time, the temporary character 'stimulated people not to put things off'. Later, a need for structure developed. As the temporary situation dragged on, the Interim Use seemed increasingly to have something permanent about it. The long-term tenants, who by a certain point had been there for years, started looking towards a situation that offered them some security of tenure. Temporariness was no longer a leitmotif in all respects, particularly now that the urban district had decided the Interim Use was to be replaced by a definitive one. Still, the inherent clash between 'temporary' and 'definitive' did the Westergasfabriek no harm. The years from 1995 to 1999, in which everyone and everything seemed to have found their place, may in retrospect be seen as the most successful period of the Interim Use, even though the charm of the temporary situation, with its lightheartedness and energy, had waned somewhat.

Returning to September 1995: that month, the unexpected news came that the IJsbreker coalition's planned move to the Westergasfabriek was not to be. The city had offered the IJsbreker an alternative location on the River IJ, at Oostelijke Handelskade, and this was a bolt out of the blue to the urban district. At one blow, the main pillar under the future plans of the Westerfabriek was gone. The fury of district council chairman Ruud Grondel was understandable – if played up a little, for it might help the city understand that they now had a debt to settle with the urban district. In any case, at the bottom of their heart not everyone was unhappy with the demise of the IJsbreker plan. De IJsbreker had already been accused of showing little interest in the unique qualities of the monumental buildings while the plans were being developed. The urban district now had a free hand to determine the future use of the Westergasfabriek. Circumstances differed considerably from those prevailing four years earlier, when the newly established district council sent out its appeal for ideas. Nearly three years of the Interim Use had shown that the complex was a viable business proposition, even without having a single major user. No new call for ideas was thus necessary decide what use of the site might take the place of the IJsbreker coalition; that use had after all proved its case already in the period since 1993.

The Westergasfabriek project team which had meanwhile been installed eagerly set to work to define its new lines of action. The city, which as said still owed the district something of a debt, was under pressure to back the urban

Westergasfabriek Developmen
Plan, 199

district's efforts. Besides financial support, the district needed a 'project alderman' on the central city council who would take overall responsibility for the project. The Amsterdam City Council assented to this and appointed Edgar Peer, the alderman for economic affairs, as the project alderman for the Westergasfabriek.

Peer proved himself an effective administrator – a man with whom you could do business. But he was not prepared to give way to the district on everything they might ask of him. It was due to Peer, for example, that 3,500 square metres of new buildings were to be erected on the Westergasfabriek site as a contribution to employment opportunities in the city. Grondel, the district councillor with the Westergasfabriek portfolio, described Peer's demand as 'a bitter-tasting diktat' but reconciled himself to it because it did no real harm to future prospects of the Westergasfabriek. The same was true of another condition Peer tied to the city's support: the district must not keep the work of refurbishing and operating the buildings to itself, but must place it in the hands of a 'private enterprise', i.e. a property developer.

From here onwards, the plan development process ran smoothly, and within a few months it was apparent that the IJsbreker's pull-out had in effect operated as a catalyst. In the same period, moreover, the deadlocked discussions around the soil cleanup were finally resolved with an outcome that was even more favourable to the urban district than the isolation-plus variant that the Ministry of Housing, Spatial Planning and the Environment had blocked for so long. The Amsterdam Environment Department had succeeded in convincing the ministry that a completely sealed layer over the contaminated soil was not even necessary, and that it would be sufficient to spread a layer of clean topsoil on those parts not covered with tarmac. Not only would this be much cheaper, it was thought, but the buildings could remain in use during the cleanup (although the last was to prove over-optimistic).

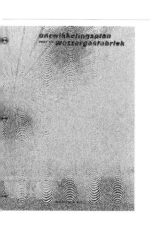

Now that the project had the wind in its sails, it was time for decisive action. A 'step by step' plan for selecting an architect for the park was completed in February 1996. Two months later, this was followed the draft of the Development Plan which later, in its final form, was to be passed by the district council. The Development Plan has since proved its worth as a guideline for the Westergasfabriek project. It combines and wherever possible attunes all the relevant aspects: the park, the soil cleanup, the buildings, the future uses, the financing and the position of the private enterprise partner then still to be sought. Not everything could be set down in detail in the Development Plan, and inevitably it had to be updated frequently after 1996. Yet now, years later, it must be recognized as a document that definitively set the course of development of the new Westergasfabriek.

On 20 December 1999, the Westergasfabriek Gasholder was the scene of a noteworthy event. Amid the tents and stalls of the *Winterparade*, two people took their places on a rotating platform. They were Mrs. Timmermans-Kuiken, the secretary of the Urban District of Westerpark, and Mr. Van Zeijl, a director of the real estate development company MAB. After two years of negotiations, the collaboration between the urban district and the real estate developer could now be sealed with a contract. The ceremony took some time for every page had to bear their signatures; but once the pens were laid down, the step was irreversible. The two parties had undertaken significant obligations towards each other: the urban district was to transfer ownership of the Westergasfabriek buildings to MAB, and the latter would then restore them and make them fit for cultural applications, as specified in the Development Plan of 1996.

Midway through the 1990s, it was Edgar Peer, the Westergasfabriek project alderman on the city council, who instigated the district to place the development of the buildings in the hands of a private company. Peer, as the chairman of the city Economic Affairs committee, was a strong proponent of a greater role for the private sector. It was moreover a period when privatization was still in vogue. The district councillor with the Westergasfabriek portfolio, Ruud Grondel, originally hoped the buildings would be developed by the district itself. But the district and the city soon agreed that the expertise of a real estate developer would be invaluable, and in any case it would be possible to stipulate conditions that would make sure the Westergasfabriek buildings remained dedicated to cultural uses.

Signature of agreement of cooperation between the District of Westerpark and the real estate development company MAB, December 1999

nterprise

This conclusion found its way into Development Plan as follows: 'The district considers that the development and operation of the buildings is not a central task of the urban district organization.' A private company would have to invest money to cover the difference between the restoration costs and any subsidies such as those provided by the city Monuments Department, and then recoup this investment from the rents collected. The selection of candidate developers began shortly after publication of the Development Plan. The urban district had the help of Kolpron, a consultancy whose field includes public-private collaboration in urban projects. One of Kolpron's tasks was to draw up a financial matrix, which would indicate how high the rents would have to be to yield a reasonable profit after a relatively simple renovation exercise.

In the first instance, talks took place with twelve commercial development companies. They were asked, among other things, for their outlook on the 'cultural vision' of the Development Plan. Most of the candidates soon dropped out, in most cases because they thought the plans offered too little scope for new building. Serious discussions continued with three of the candidates. Finally, only MAB remained as the real estate developer whom the urban district most trusted to stay the course through the awkward and lengthy negotiations.

MAB was founded in 1970 by Ton Meijer, who to this day is still the owner and board chairman of the conglomerate *MAB Group* (which has operating companies in the Netherlands, Germany, France, Belgium and the UK). MAB is something of an oddity in the world of real estate developers. Unlike most development companies, it focuses sharply on complicated projects in existing urban areas. MAB is not a name one readily associates with newbuild housing projects in VINEX areas or with office complexes in high-visibility locations along the motorway. Most of their projects involve a range of functions: homes, offices, shops and, increasingly, leisure facilities. The underlying idea is that this diversity of functions makes a location – and hence the city – more attractive. For MAB, this has a double advantage: the attractiveness of the location boosts the value of the property, and at the same time the development company builds an image as a partner with the best interests of the city at heart.

MAB realized that the Westergasfabriek would raise the company's profile as a visionary developer with an eye for unusual urban situations. The project also presented an opportunity to gain experience with distinctive forms of 'leisure' – a sector in which local governments, too, have taken an increasing interest in recent years. Company owner Ton Meijer's personal enthusiasm for

art and architecture no doubt also contributed to MAB taking the plunge with the Westergasfabriek.

Not long afterwards, in May 1997, MAB showed the urban district of Westerpark that they were serious about the Westergasfabriek by signing a contract of intent. That it then took a further two and a half years to complete the negotiations indicates how tricky an affair the transfer of ownership of the buildings was. The challenge of reaching agreement and setting everything down in writing was hard enough. The district wanted assurance that the use of the buildings would accord with the outlook of the Development Plan. The new owners could not be allowed to do whatever they liked with the buildings, and the same certainty must apply even if MAB were to sell the buildings to a third-party investor after finishing their development work. Similar concerns applied to the setting of maximum rents on the basis of Kolpron's matrix. The rents must be profitable but they must not be allowed to rise to a level unaffordable to ten-

**Westergasfabriek as
a storage facility for
the Municipal Energy Company**

ants from the cultural sector. Much diplomatic skill was also needed to reach a viable agreement on the consequences of the soil pollution.

Neither party was well acquainted with the field of action for the negotiations. MAB felt at home with offices and shops but had no experience of the rather chaotic cultural world of the Westergasfabriek. Matters like 'incidental letting', which has since clearly emerged as the most profitable business aspect of the Westergasfabriek, necessitated thorough research. Naturally, too, each party hoped to come out of the negotiations with the greatest possible advantage. An urban district that wished to establish the designated cultural function as firmly as possible without running too many financial risks thus had to reach agreement with a real estate development company which wished to be burdened with the least possible restrictions.

It was late 1999 by the time MAB and the urban district were at one about the conditions for handover of the buildings. The urban district's commitment to create the park was set off against MAB's commitment to make the buildings suitable for their designated function and to build 3,500 square metres of new buildings. Since the district would no longer manage the buildings, alternative measures had to be taken. MAB set up a management and operating company for this purpose in 2000 – a full MAB subsidiary which went under the name of Westergasfabriek BV. Liesbeth Jansen, who had organized the Interim Use since 1992, became its managing director.

The collaboration agreement required the district to issue two offers for the ground lease – one for the existing buildings and one for the new buildings. Special conditions, which were also stated in the agreement, were attached to the ground lease. One of these conditions laid down the designated cultural use, together with supporting functions: for example, it was determined that six large-scale events could take place annually, and that neighbourhood organizations would be allowed to let one of the building spaces once per annum for half the normal rent.

The soil pollution issues seemed to have been dealt with satisfactorily in a number of clear-cut understandings. By providing 'vapour-proof' floors, MAB would indemnify itself against all claims regarding possible consequences of pollution under the buildings. Conversely, the owner would have no claims against the urban district for any consequences of soil pollution, subject to the condition that the urban district took effective measures to decontaminate the open areas.

The financial aspects of the agreement were based on the assumption that MAB would receive two appreciable subsidies: 2.4 million euros in historic buildings subsidy, and 1.8 million euros in the form of an 'ICES' contribution (ICES being a Dutch government programme to improve the economic structure). MAB would have to match the total of 4 million euros in subsidies by paying a roughly similar amount to the urban district: over two million euros to buy

off the ground rent for 100 years, plus 1.7 million euros as a contribution to creating the park. It thus appeared that MAB would be receiving the buildings as a free gift, although the company actually also committed itself to investing further millions in the restoration work. According to the financial matrix, the specified figures would finally generate an initial gross yield of eight percent per annum.

Incorporating the stipulations for the handover – in particular, regarding the cultural designation of the buildings – into the ground lease allowed the urban district to rest assured that these conditions would apply equally to future owners. Still, a one-hundred year lease could curb the designated use of the buildings only in very general terms. The lease moreover provided no control over the use of the outdoor areas, which remained in the hands of the urban district. A new urban zoning plan was therefore required, so that the stipulations could be elaborated in fuller detail and expanded to designate the use of the outdoor areas. Like the collaboration agreement, the 'Westerpark ABC Zoning Plan' (in which the letters A, B and C denote the subplans of the Westerpark) cites the Westergasfabriek Development Plan explicitly as its basis.

Once all the plans were ready in early 2000 (apart from the zoning plan, then still faced with lengthy procedure that would not be all plain sailing), it became possible to sign the 'deed of lease assignment' on 6 March. The transfer of ownership of the Westergasfabriek buildings to MAB was now accomplished.

So it came about that a private company developed the buildings with the aim of exploiting them commercially for cultural uses. In other words, the Westergasfabriek fitted into the new picture of relations between business and the arts – two worlds that used to have little mutual affinity. It was not until the nineteen eighties, when the free market philosophy began to make headway in

Hannes Wallrafen,
artist's project

society at large, that people began to accept the idea that the market and culture might have more to offer each other than previously thought. Even then,
within the market framework, 'cultural' developments were stimulated by non-
market means such as subsidies. A distinction was often made in some sectors
such as theatre between subsidized and 'free' or non-subsidized productions.
The free productions were at first looked down upon in the subsidized, 'serious'
theatre circles – an indication that there were still barriers dividing the market
from culture. And although breaches were gradually being made in those
barriers, for example through the sponsoring of museums and concert halls,
the response from the public and the cultural sector was at first somewhat
sceptical.

Resistance to the free-market approach to the arts gradually declined during the nineteen nineties. 'Cultural entrepreneurship' became a widely accept-
ed (if not always uncontroversial) concept; it was, for example, one of the key

Recording of Marco Borsato
video clip with Sita,
'Walking on Water'

Advertising on Gasholder in
1980s

themes in the Dutch Cultural Policy of 1999 issued under the then Secretary of State for Culture, Mr. Van der Ploeg. It seemed by then that a firm relationship had been established between the arts and the market: the artist had become an entrepreneur, with an eye for the market and with a commercially viable outfit.

On closer consideration, however, things were not that simple. The supposed marriage of culture and the economy resulted in just as many gross oversimplifications as did the former belief in an absolute antithesis. Culture and economics might well have countless points of contact, but that is quite a different thing from being on the same wavelength. There are cases where it makes sense to view culture as an economic activity, but there are just as many situations where market laws are scarcely relevant. Everyone understands that a ticket for a performance in the Concertgebouw is more expensive than for one by a local musical society. People are prepared to pay more for better cultural products but the converse is not necessarily true. The fact that a pop concert draws a bigger audience than a poetry reading does not imply a proportionate difference in their cultural value. That is why the arts need financial support in the form of subsidies and sponsoring.

It is not the purpose of this book to reproduce the subtle analysis needed to show where and how culture and the market have moved closer together. However, I can cite two areas where this is unmistakably so – and both are relevant to the cultural use of the Westergasfabriek.

To begin with, there is a stronger market orientation on the part of institutions and companies in the cultural sector. These are growing increasingly aware that they need to operate in a more businesslike fashion. This is indeed what is primarily meant by cultural entrepreneurship: that culture makers set to work in the most economically efficient way possible, by taking pains to reduce costs and generate income. This implies, among other things, paying greater attention to business management and to raising funds from sources other than the usual subsidies.

Receptiveness to the market is literally evident in the professional concern that many cultural organizations show for marketing. Their aim is not of course to submit uncritically to the dictate of the market, but to gain an understanding of their audience and to motivate that audience to 'consume' their cultural products. Cultural entrepreneurship must thus not be interpreted as letting the profit motive overshadow the arts. Substantial profits are rarely made in most cultural activities; and in some cases any profit that is made must be deducted from the subsidy receivable.

The second kind of cultural entrepreneurship relates to the person of the cultural entrepreneur – an adventurous individual who is prepared to explore new roads, to reconnoitre regions as yet untouched. It was already clear during the Interim Use that the Westergasfabriek presented fertile ground for enterprises of this kind.

It looks as though the Westergasfabriek will soon once more be a good location for both types of cultural entrepreneurship. The market-level rents will be affordable only to those cultural tenants who run their company or institution in a businesslike fashion, and assuming something of the free and easy atmosphere of the Interim Use period can be revived, the Westergasfabriek will once more offer a good climate for cultural adventures.

The greater receptiveness of the cultural sector towards the market has another side to it. This is the increased relevance of the arts to the economy in general. In a city like Amsterdam, which is the capital of the Netherlands in cultural as well as other respects, a substantial proportion of the professional population earns its bread and butter in the cultural sector. But culture's economic importance goes further. The cultural climate and the range of cultural amenities is a significant motive for people – especially those of higher educational backgrounds – to move to the city. This leads in turn to a labour market which is attractive to companies that in themselves have little to do with the cultural sector. Commercial enterprises are keen to develop a 'cultural' image, and this aspiration may take the form of the sponsoring of cultural organizations and events.

Culture is just one part of the leisure industry, a sector involving considerable amounts of money in its own right. But culture is perhaps considered even more significant as a catalyst for economic developments in a broader field. That cities and real estate developers are so interested in leisure as an aspect of urban development programmes is not so much for the immediate profits to be made as because it helps make locations more attractive. The financial advantage resides in the higher property prices and higher rents for homes and commercial premises in the vicinity. Culture may be regarded as a 'higher' form of leisure: it is no mere coincidence that the area around Museumplein, the recently remodelled square around which the Concertgebouw and the main art museums are grouped, has become one of Amsterdam's most sought-after locations for residential and office space.

For real estate developers, investments in leisure serve primarily to raise the value of other components – particularly housing and office buildings – in multifunctional projects. The Westergasfabriek, however, is not multifunctional, at least not in the sense of forming part of a combination with more conventional (and, for investors, more familiar) functions such as homes and offices. If the cultural functions have the effect of boosting the value of the Westergasfabriek's immediate surroundings, it will not be MAB (or their successors as owners) who pluck the fruits, but those who are lucky enough to own houses or business premises in the vicinity. MAB never reckoned on earning a fortune through the Westergasfabriek; on the contrary, they expected a profit somewhat lower than that usually yielded by real estate development projects.

MAB had other motives for taking the plunge with the Westergasfabriek. In relation to their whole portfolio, it was a fairly modest-sized project on which they could afford to take a little risk. The company sees the Westergasfabriek as a testing-ground for exploring new tasks, tasks of a kind they expect will become more important to them in the near future. The Westergasfabriek has enabled MAB to study how part of a city can be made to flourish, with limited resources and with appealing, if not specifically commercial, functions.

A second motive for MAB's involvement was closely related to the above. The MAB group aimed to promote itself as a brand, as a 'developer for the city'. By adorning the cover of their annual report not with gleaming office towers or stylish apartment developments, but with a restored and revitalized gasworks, the company wished to distinguish itself in the eyes of its potential clients (who are mostly city councils) as a public-spirited, 'cultural' developer. Through the Westergasfabriek, MAB demonstrated its affinity with the leisure sector, and in particular with its highest form, namely culture.

Soil cleanup for construction of
Broadway

Apart from these considerations, MAB had as yet no idea what was facing them. If the board of directors in their headquarters in The Hague had any inkling, they might perhaps never have started. Fortunately for the Westergasfabriek (in a manner of speaking) the problems did not emerge until later when there was no way back for either MAB or the urban district.

The first setbacks can be put down to unforeseen complications in the soil decontamination work. Until the transfer of ownership to MAB, everyone assumed that most of the buildings could stay in use during the cleanup period. People referred optimistically to the 'happy building pit', and there was a plan to release camels onto the sandy wastes of the site. The Interim Use was expected to merge more or less smoothly into a definitive situation, thereby giving the renewed Westergasfabriek a flying start. But when the urban district and MAB were on the point of starting construction of the park and renovation of the buildings, several skeletons tumbled simultaneously out of the closet.

It appeared, for example, that the ground under the buildings was more severely polluted in some places than earlier research (with a limited number of random test drillings) had indicated. Pits left behind after the removal of machine foundations turned out to contain heavily contaminated waste. In the contract between MAB and the urban district, everyone had assumed that the nature of the pollution under the buildings was irrelevant because the ground was to be sealed off with 'vapour proof' concrete floors. The discovery of a number of pollution hot spots undermined this assumption. MAB faced additional expense not only because of the special standards required of the concrete and the seals, but also because their employees would have to work in protective 'space suits' under stringent safety rules.

Other discoveries of hitherto unknown pollution concentrations admittedly took place outside the buildings, but they did make the use of the buildings increasingly difficult and eventually as good as impossible. Toxic tar was found

A self-supporting tent was
erected as a safety measure
during decontamination of the
gasholder foundations

in the foundations of the former retort house, where the Events Field was
supposed to be realized. Much worse consequences transpired when the
cover of one of the water-filled gasholder bases was broken open. As the
rubble tumbled into the sludge below, a revolting stench arose: nobody had
known that the basement was used as a waste dump while the gasworks
still operated.

Following these unpleasant discoveries, workers in chemical protection
suits became an increasingly frequent sight in the Westergasfabriek. Fences
were erected around the Purifier Building early in 2001, and work in the
Supervisors' Houses and the Transformer House had to be halted. The situation
gradually became intolerable for those tenants who were still using the buildings, and they all left the site by mid 2002. The only places still open to the public were the West Pacific café-restaurant and the Ketelhuis cinema. The 'happy
building pit' had turned out to be wishful thinking.

Temporary purification
equipment for ground
decontamination

Cleanup work in one of the
gasholder foundations

Another reverse for MAB was the result of an appeal against the zoning plan launched by the Friends of the Westerpark and the neighbourhood centre. The appellants argued that, in view of the expected volume of visitors, an environmental impact assessment must be carried out; and the Council of State broadly agreed with them. The Council of State did allow extension of the building permits for those structures that were in such a poor state as to make restoration urgent, such as the Purifier Building. MAB, however, wished for the security of a new zoning plan before preparing these buildings for their new use. Other components of the project, such as renovation of the Transformer Building and the new buildings around the Gasholder and in the Cité des Arts, would in any case have to wait for the environmental impact statement and the new zoning plan.

These setbacks together added up to years of delay in the restoration of the buildings and hence in the arrival of tenants. MAB suffered considerable losses, due not only to missed rent income but also to rising building costs since 1999 (the year of the 'financial matrix') and to enhanced Dutch safety standards following the disasters in Enschede and Volendam.

MAB had meanwhile learned that a cultural project like the Westergasfabriek was too unusual to attract the interest of other private investors. Because MAB is an independent real estate developer without links to a financing company, it needs two other kinds of enterpreneur: a financier to provide funding for the period until the project is sold, and an investor who will eventually become the owner of the project.

The banks thought the Westergasfabriek project so high-risk, particularly while no private investor was within sight, that they were unwilling to back it except at high interest rates. This implied further rises in MAB's costs, which had already risen considerably. Eventually a solution appeared in the form of a loan from the National Restoration Fund. Without this loan on favourable terms,

leanup in basement of former
etort House

MAB would probably be unable to rent out the buildings at the agreed rates, which would seriously jeopardize the intended cultural application of the Westergasfabriek.

The National Restoration Fund did attach one proviso to their loan: the urban district had to stand guarantee. This necessitated a further series of long and sometimes thorny negotiations between the urban district and MAB in the first half of 2003. The urban district had assumed that the financial side of the deal was concluded on transfer of ownership of the buildings to MAB; and the required guarantee entailed a further, if small, financial risk. Conversely, MAB had some reason to feel let down by the setbacks in soil pollution and by the Council of State's decision on the zoning plan. The district had an interest in MAB being able to uphold the designated use of the Westergasfabriek with the aid of the National Restoration Fund loan.

On 29 July 2003, an agreement on the municipal guarantee between MAB and the urban district was sealed by the official deposition of no less than twelve documents. This mass of paper was justified because the guarantee negotiations presented an opportunity to resolve various issues that had remained unclear in the agreement of three years earlier, such as a closing date for investments.

The delay in development has resulted in the Westergasfabriek presenting very different picture in 2003 to the optimistic nineties and the period of Interim Use. The former tenants have been biding their time in provisional accommodation such as old school buildings until they are able to return to the buildings. For some of them, the wait has been too long. Orkater, the theatre company that perhaps more than any other tenant set the mood of the Westergasfabriek, has found alternative permanent accommodation in an industrial area in a nearby former docks area. Not only had the Westergasfabriek meanwhile become too

Renovation of Gasholder roof

expensive for them, but Orkater and MAB were unable to reach agreement about the eventual facilities of the building.

Apart from present worries, however, and although later than intended, there are prospects that an energy will develop in and around the buildings as exciting as before. The plans for the operating company Westergasfabriek BV are as good as ready – apart from some details which cannot yet be filled in. It is not yet known, for example, what structure will be appropriate for the business operation; neither is it clear what limitations will apply to the operating company programming some of the activities itself (rather than leaving them entirely to the decisions of long-term and short-term users).

The new situation will have both marked similarities and marked differences compared to the Interim Use period. The main differences concern the level of aspirations. Having a profit-making operation – the choice made by the urban district when it decided to convey the buildings to a market party – dictates considerably higher rents than those charged in the old situation (although those rents could hardly have been made any higher considering the shortness of the contracts and the condition the buildings were in at the time).

The upper and lower limits for future rents were established in the financial matrix that formed part of the agreement between MAB and the district. The permitted ranges allow MAB some scope to bring the yield on their investment up to par, after the setbacks of recent years. For example, MAB presently bases the rent only on the shell of the building, which means that tenants will have to pay further charges for furnishings, fittings and services. For a starting cultural entrepreneur with little financial room for manoeuvre, the Westergasfabriek buildings will no doubt be too expensive. This kind of user will have to seek refuge in abandoned factories etc., buildings that resemble the Westergasfabriek of 1992. (It is a problem, though, that Amsterdam is gradually running out of such low-priced options.)

The future tenants of the Westergasfabriek will thus need a fairly solid financial basis. The Westergasfabriek will probably soon no longer be a venue for initiatives that have to prove themselves from the ground up. Not that this excludes the possibility of a different kind of breeding ground: a location whose climate is a stimulus to new, unexpected cultural activities. There is scope for rent differentials to make this possible. Tenants who have less money to work with but are considered important to the cultural climate could be asked to pay a little less than the standard rent. This would be offset by higher rents for more profitable functions. A scheme like this would not be unique; shopping centres, too, try to tempt 'pace setters' to set up shop by offering them advantageous leases.

The *Utilization Plan* adopted by Westergasfabriek BV is based on what is termed 'a healthy business basis'. Its starting points are the master plan, which describes the spatial organization of functions, and the business plan of Westergasfabriek BV. A constant theme is to achieve as much variety as possible. The utilization plan calls for many combinations of elements which reinforce one another precisely because they are so different. It starts with the combination of cultural activities with the park, which is primarily an everyday amenity for residents of the adjacent areas. Then, as many possible differences are sought within the cultural activities. The combination of permanent tenants and incidental users will provide continuity and recognizability in combination with variation and surprise. There will always be Dutch films on show in the Ketelhuis (or another building designated to that purpose); in the Gasholder, on the other hand, a circus might well make way for a dance party.

Besides the public activities, the Westergasfabriek will offer room to cultural enterprises that do their work in relative seclusion. And people arriving to attend a performance or event will rub shoulders with those merely enjoying the atmosphere from comfort of the pavement café.

The Westergasfabriek will also accommodate a variety of art forms – not only theatre but music, fashion, film and visual art. There will be room both for mass-audience events such as a concert by a popular singer like André Hazes or a house party, and for speciality art forms that attract much smaller audiences. All the same, the number of mass-audience events will be restricted to avoid overburdening the local population.

Diversity in areas such as the above has to be content-managed to a certain extent. It is one of the criteria that plays a part in the selection of tenants (just as is an 'adventurous' character and the possibility that the tenant will provide links to valuable networks). Besides this passive form of content management in which diversity is left to the tenants, the Westergasfabriek will take an active role by programming a number of cultural events itself.

The master plan compiled by Francine Houben of Mecanoo architecten provides a basis for the spatial distribution of the activities. There will be four clusters. The buildings between the Haarlemmervaart canal and the Events Field make up *The Village*. The largest of this group is the Purifier Building, which will contain among other things a 'morning and afternoon' café, art galleries, offices and studios for cultural enterprises, plus a hall of monumental proportions for theatre productions, fashion shows and other events. The Regulator House, adjacent to the lifting bridge, will contain the offices of Westergasfabriek BV, including the central information and ticket desk. Among the buildings to the north of the Purifier Building are the Machine Building, which is being adapted for incidental letting, and the two small Metering Buildings, which will house small-scale public functions such as a kiosk, toilets and deckchair rental. It is still unknown whether the Dutch Cinema will stay in the Ketelhuis or move to the Purifier Building.

The *Spektakeldorp* ('Spectacular Village') consists of the Gasholder and Transformer Building. This will be the venue for large-scale events. The Gasholder is the biggest space in the Westergasfabriek and is destined, accord-

Master Plan,
Mecanoo architecten

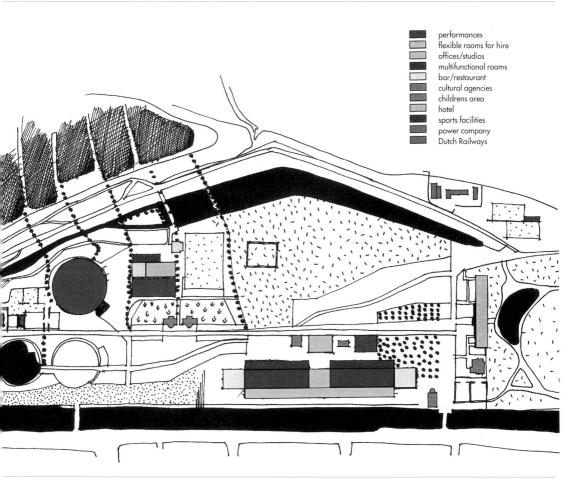

performances
flexible rooms for hire
offices/studios
multifunctional rooms
bar/restaurant
cultural agencies
childrens area
hotel
sports facilities
power company
Dutch Railways

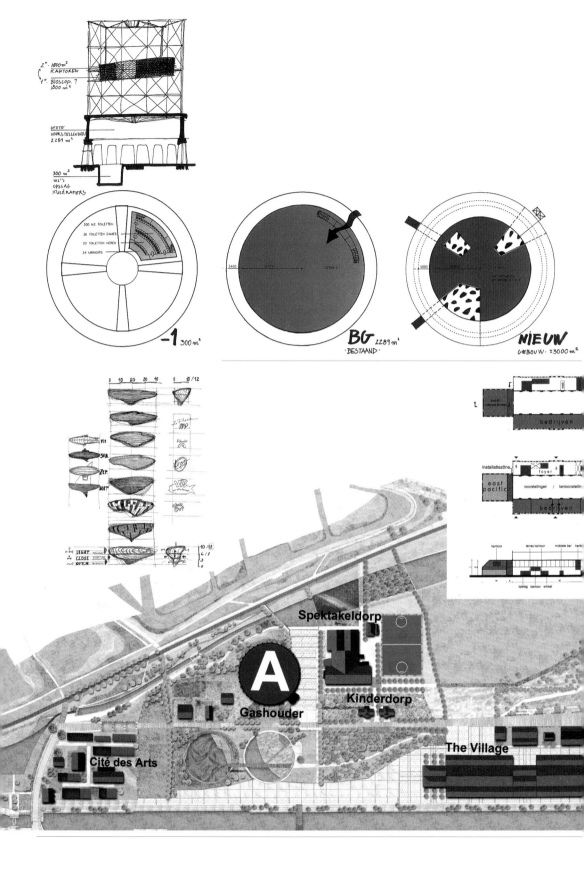

ing to the utilization plan, to become again 'the biggest magnet for attention, publicity and identity'. The Gasholder will house special events such as operas, fairs, product launches and corporate celebrations. The Transformer Building, where Toneelgroep Amsterdam used to perform, will be dedicated once more to theatre productions.

The *Kinderdorp* ('Children's Village') is the smallest of the clusters. Activities for children, possibly plus a catering function, will make use of the two Supervisors' Houses. Finally, the extreme western point of the Westergasfabriek site will be the place of the *Cité des Arts*, which will consist mainly of new buildings. The number of audience-attracting functions will be limited there, and most of the buildings will serve as offices for cultural enterprises.

Ideas by Mecanoo architecten for the Gasholder

Design involving reconstruction of the Gasholder to its original height of 13.5 metres. A large sculptural object suspended from the supporting frame, symbolizing the transition from gasworks to 'culture factory'.

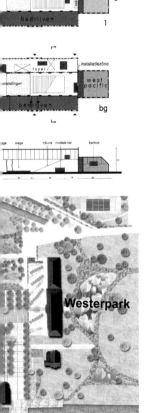

Once the district council approved the development plan for the new Westergasfabriek in 1996, it was time for detailed planning and design work to begin. The biggest task would be designing the new park, and the soil cleanup operation had to be planned in close coordination with the park construction. And even though the development plan referred to the buildings needing 'fabric repairs', an architect was required to assist with the renovation. The programme also included 3,500 square metres of newbuild space. Finally, to ensure that the plan components – the park and the buildings – matched up, a comprehensive master plan was required.

The procedure for selecting a designer for the park was already set out in the development plan. First, a 'park working group', which included three local residents, was to draw up a list of twelve candidate landscape architects. Once the latter had made presentations to the committee, five of them were chosen (with assent of the district council) to take part in a limited competition. The competition shortlist consisted of Michael van Gessel, Adriaan Geuze, Kathryn Gustafson, Edwin Santhagens and Lodewijk Wiegersma.

The five shortlisted landscape architects were each asked to prepare a vision – not yet a detailed design – on the basis of principles defined in the development plan. These principles were that the grounds were to have 'a green, recreational park function', that local residents and the tenants of the buildings would be the main users, that natural environmental qualities had to be strengthened and that the park must include a space for open-air events of over one hectare in area.

As hoped, the five designers showed that these principles were capable of generating a variety of design concepts. The proposals by Van Gessel and by Santhagens both drew a distinction between a large, free space and, disposed within it, a number of detached objects (buildings and gardens) to meet the more specific programme components. The park concepts by Gustafson and Geuze were both relatively traditional with plenty of greenery. Wiegersma's plan was substantially green, too, but its choice of a limited range of formal elements made it simpler in layout.

A judging committee of experts (landscape architects, an architectural historian and a planning specialist, under the chairmanship of a communications consultant) had the task of consulting with local residents' organizations and then recommending a final choice of the landscape architect. Their decided to plump for Kathryn Gustafson, the only foreign entrant, 'because the plan is

designs

The plan by **Kathryn Gustafson** (in collaboration with Francine Houben of Mecanoo architecten) is titled *Changement*. She proposed a park that promises varying experiences both in space and time (the changing seasons). The park changes in character from west to east: from a rather formal urban park to a freer design with more scope for nature. Although a contemporary park design concept, it also has something classical, with traditional ingredients like a large meadow, water features, woods, flower beds, an orchard and a central axis.

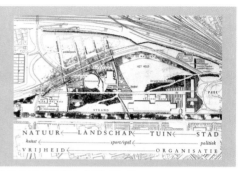

By titling his plan *Parkfabriek* (Park Factory), **Michael van Gessel** made it clear he intended to take advantage of the distinctive factory atmosphere. The root of his concept is a contrast between two worlds: a tough, open outside world and a relatively refined inside world. The buildings belong to that inside world, along with a series of enclosed 'park chambers' with distinctive atmospheres and programmes. Van Gessel's outside world sets itself off against the inside one in a formation of public squares and drives of various sizes, capable of being used in countless different ways. The outside world is fully paved with a variety of materials, most of them recycled. An abundance of trees is meant to convey an impression of the former industrial site being reclaimed by nature.

Lodewijk Wiegersma describes his plan *Bomen/Beelden* (Trees/Sculptures) as 'profusely green, with lots of trees and grass'. The basic structure of the park is clear and simple: a diagonal axis runs from the western extremity of the site to the boundary with the old Westerpark, to the north of the district council offices. In the middle, between the Gasholder and the Purification Building, there is a central square. The Events Field is located in the north-eastern quarter. The northern zone of the park has room for nature development. There are no paths, for everyone must find his or her own way. The diagonal arrangement produces a contrast between the green elements – mainly avenues of trees and trimmed hedges – and the buildings.

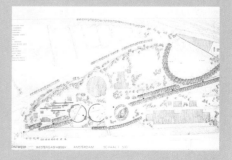

The name **Edwin Santhagens** gave his plan, *Het Vrije Veld* ('The Free Field') refers to a concept in which most of the site is open space without explicit functions. The specific functional programmes are concentrated into the buildings and a

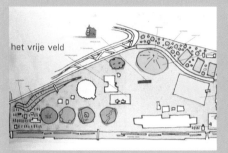

number of thematic gardens, which are arranged as separate objects in the space. Examples of the thematic gardens are an ecological pond, a sunbathing hill, an orchard and a sports lawn. The Free Field is paved over half its area with golden yellow stone chippings and has no prominent furniture or fixtures. However, there are some spotlights to illuminate the buildings sunk into the ground at various points.

The name *Park en Plein* (Park and Square) gives an idea of what **Adriaan Geuze** intended with his design: a distinctly green zone surrounding a rectangular square in the middle of the new, expanded Westerpark. Most of the buildings

adjoin this square; only the Gasholder is encircled by greenery. The square is the location for large-scale activities like festivals, celebrations, exhibitions or carnivals. It is paved with materials already available on the site. The boundary between the square and the green park is marked by a 'charismatic fence'.

contemporary and at the same time arouses much confidence for the future detailing and execution'. The urban district of Westerpark voted to adopt the jury's verdict, and Gustafson thus won the commission to design the new park.

Kathryn Gustafson was born in the town of Yakima (Washington, USA) in 1951. After training as a fashion designer in New York, she moved to Paris in the nineteen seventies. It was not until she had spent a period there designing garments and textiles that her passion for landscape architecture began to emerge. She went to Versailles to study the new subject. France was to remain her home for nearly a quarter of a century, so she must be regarded as a French rather than an American landscape architect. Nonetheless, she returned to her native Washington State where she set up a third office in Seattle in the late nineties. Besides her firm in Paris, she had already established a practice in London together with the architect Neil Porter. Shortly afterwards, she abandoned the

French operation altogether. The work on the Westergasfabriek project will take place in London, with Porter in day-to-day charge.

In France, Gustafson earned fame with designs for the open spaces around the headquarter offices of large companies like Shell, Esso and L'Oréal, for Place des Droits de l'Homme in the Paris suburb of Evry, and for *Jardins de l'Imainaire* in Terrasson. It was not until recent years that she began to draw attention with projects in other countries, among them the redesign of Crystal Palace Park in London, the *Ross Terrace* for the Museum of Natural History in New York, the *Shoulder Garden* in Chicago and the master plan for the Museum of Fine Arts in Boston. Gustafson had her most prestigious commission to date in 2002, when she won the competition for the Princess Diana Memorial in Hyde Park, London. She moreover won the Chrysler Design Award the previous year.

Gustafson's work often finds itself in a borderland between landscape architecture and land art. She herself characterizes it as both poetic and rational (she attributes the poetical side to her English mother and the rationality to her Swedish father). Her designs have a robust structure although it is sometimes disguised by more fluid forms. Gustafson aims to make people connect through their senses to a landscape that has the character of a sculpture; her 'fountain gardens' in Terrasson are an impressive illustration of this. It is not for nothing that the book about her French work is titled *Sculpting the Land*.

After Gustafson was commissioned to produce a park design on the basis of her winning vision for the Westergasfabriek site, she elaborated her original concept thoroughly, modifying it where necessary. Yet the park as built has remained close to her original competition entry. The main scheme is the same and what modifications there are may be regarded as elaborations or refinements.

**Provisional park design by
Katryn Gustafson**

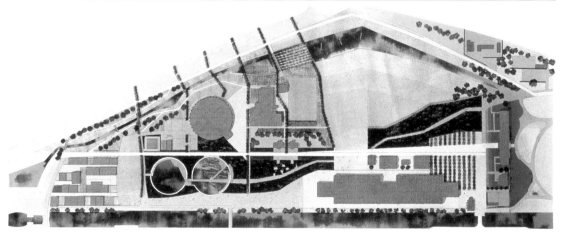

Definitive park design

The park has more height variations than at first, for example. Gustafson was helped in this respect by the stipulation for all excavated soil to remain within the confines of the site. Other differences from the competition design are that two ponds instead of one have been made in the foundations of former gas-holders, and the 'Broadway' (called 'the path of dreams' in the competition design) runs between these Gasholder Ponds to the sculpture field. The descending quay towards the Haarlemmervaart (called 'the beach') in the com-petition design is replaced by a raised grassy embankment with trees, and grass replaces pavement in the sculpture field. This last change was made to satisfy the residents' organizations, who wished for 'less stone and more green-ery'.

The plan has also been modified in a few respect on the north side of the central axis. A korfball pitch has been added, and what was little more than a meandering stream in the competition entry has developed into a clever system

of water gardens and water terraces. Gustafson's original idea of extending
several avenues of trees out into the polder, to the north of the bicycle path,
could not be implemented because the land concerned lies outside the Westergasfabriek area.

The design's underlying general structure has been accentuated in the park as
built. The title Gustafson gave her design, *Changement*, must be primarily interpreted as a reference to the way the park changes in character from east to
west. In the east, around the district council offices, the layout is related to that
of a traditional, formal city park. The plant selection emphasis is here on cultiv-
ated species, whereas towards the western end more native species have been
chosen. In the middle area, we can recognize hints of park designs of the nineteen fifties and sixties, which were primarily concerned with recreation. The
landscape concept that typifies the seventies and eighties, with its stress on

Park under construction

nature and ecology, lies to the northwest of the new park proper, in the Over-brakerpolder. The contemporary approach is most evident in the Westergas-fabriek site itself – in the idea of regarding the landscape as a confrontation between humanity and nature. This outlook is most clearly expressed in the water garden, where the selection of plants (both native and exotic) and the maintenance they require both imply a combination of deliberate intervention and giving nature a free rein.

A characteristic of Gustafson's work is the combination of a strong, clear main structure with delicate detailing in which each place has a distinctive atmosphere. The basis of this structure was already present, in the form of the existing buildings and the elongated quay alongside the Haarlemmervaart canal. As a forceful line in the same direction, Gustafson added the central axis. She decided not to continue this axis between the Purifier Building and the smaller buildings to its northwest – which might seem the obvious thing to do

Construction of the ribbon pool

Plastic matting used to reinforce
the turf of the Events Field

at first sight – but to keep it above the built-up area. The axis thus becomes a boundary between two worlds: the stony world of the buildings in the south, and the green world of the woods and the Events Field to the north. The central axis now extends under the portal of the district council offices and through the old Westerpark.

A counterpoint to the central axis is offered by the Broadway. This path (like its New York namesake) follows the direction of the main structure, but is permitted an angular deflection here and there. The Broadway is not only more capricious, but also narrower and more intimate, than the central axis; it runs for the most part through planted woodlands.

The clear, long lines of the main structure allowed Gustafson to diversify the individual park component areas more widely. There are open and enclosed spaces, green and paved areas, and natural and visibly artificial elements. People can thus interact socially in a huge diversity of spots. Particular plant

Planting the new park

3D models

species are associated with specific places, so that every part of the park has a unique planting scheme. As a consequence, there are no less than 62 different kinds of tree, 100 kinds of shrub, 130 border plants, 19 wetland plant species, 14 ferns and 23 different flowering bulbs.

7 September 2003:
The park opens to the public

The **central axis** is the main access route for the park. The granite paving along its full length give the central axis unity, while it nonetheless offers a variety of visual experiences. The central axis grows narrower towards the west, producing an accentuated perspective effect.

Between the Market Square and the Events Field, there is the **Hill**. The Broadway passes eastwards over this hill and through a wood. On the margin of the wood, along the central axis, there are three semi-concealed spaces described as 'reading rooms'.

The **North Plaza**, covered with yellow gravel, is the place where the old and the new parks meet. Paths (among them the bicycle path and Broadway) spread out from here in all directions. This is also the starting point of the Ribbon Pool, whose banks double as park benches.

The geometrical **Ribbon Pool**, with its sharp bend at one point, forms the northern boundary of the Events Field. Owing to the pool's bed of black concrete and natural stone, it acts as a mirror for the scudding clouds that typify the Dutch skies. The long, narrow shape of the pool produces a noteworthy perspective. Children can paddle in the water of the eastern part.

The large surface are and the grand conception of the **Events Field** make it suitable for a wide variety of activities, but for most of the time it will just be a very large meadow for sunbathing and play. The anticipated intensive use necessitated high standards for the turf. A certain amount of research turned up a reinforced turf of a kind used in the practice pitches of Edinburgh rugby stadium, which serve as car parks during matches. The reinforced base of plastic matting made this meadow one of the most costly investments of the whole new park.

To the north of the Ribbon Pool, there lies the **Amphitheatre**. The grassy embankment reaches a maximum height of five metres at the angular bend. The south-facing slope makes this one of the sunniest spots in the park. It can serve as a grandstand for various events. The bicycle path and a footpath run along the margin of the first slope.

Canal promenade, section

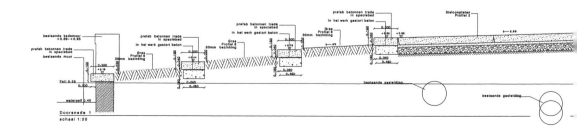

93

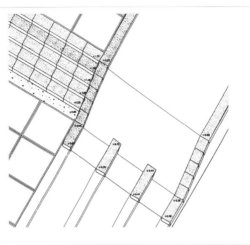

Canal promenade

Like the central axis, the **Canal Promenade** runs the full length of the park. The promenade is paved with reinforced concrete slabs and brick. Around the middle section, between the canal and the promenade proper, there is a stepped grassy field with trees; the steps can also be useful as seats.

Between the two Gasholder Ponds and *Cité des Arts* (still under construction), there is the oval **sculpture field**. The lawn of the sculpture field has a slightly convex topography and is raised above the surroundings.

The gardens of the Supervisors' Houses contain the **playgrounds** for children of various ages. Designed by Sybolt Meindertsma, they include among other things a 'hut village' and a play circuit.

The new bridge over the Haarlemmervaart leads us to the **Theatre Square**, which lies between the Gasholder and the Transformer Building. The square adjoins the water of the Theatre Pool on its north side. Cables for hanging lights and other equipment span the square.

Between the unashamedly artificial Ribbon Pool beside the Events Field and the more naturalistically designed water garden, there are three pools. From east to west, these are the **Swamp Cypress Pool**, the **Reed Pool** and the **Theatre Pool**. The **Swamp Cypress Pool** contains 36 *Taxodium* trees with their roots in the water. The Reed Pool lies to the north of the Transformer Building, and has an important function in purification of the water. Floating on the water of the Theatre Pool, there are a number of wooden decks. These make it possible to cross the pool to the open polder country on the far side.

In the **Water Garden**, an artificial stream has been constructed above the original ditch, carrying the water over several waterfalls in a westerly direction. The stream and the path alongside it are crossed by two bridges. The water garden has low, dense plantation in three areas: the White Garden (with white-flowering plants and trees), the Fern Waterfall and the Foliage Garden. The Water Garden ends at the extreme western corner of the Westergasfabriek.

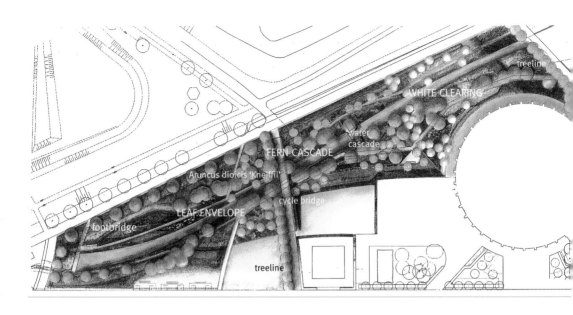

treeline

WHITE CLEARING

water
cascade

FERN CASCADE

Aruncus dioicis 'Kneiffii'

cycle bridge

LEAF ENVELOPE

footbridge

treeline

The foundations of the two long-demolished gasholders have been used to create two sunken **Gasholder Ponds**. The two ponds are linked. One has been turned into a water garden, and the other a lily pond. Visitors can descend from various directions to the wooden decks which lie just above the water surface.

The **Market Square** forms the focus of the eastern part of the Westergasfabriek. It is sited just beyond the lifting bridge, the main entrance to the new park. The square acts as a foyer for activities elsewhere in the park, but could serve well as a location for a street market or fair. The ground is covered with recycled, reinforced concrete paving slabs, plus strips of concrete and stainless steel. The orthogonal character of the market square is emphasized by a grid of magnolia trees and steel lighting columns.

Once the refurbishment of the district council offices is complete, it will have a new front garden in the form of the traditional **Rose Garden**. The formal design is a reference to the garden in the old Westerpark, on the opposite side of the council offices. The design is musically inspired; the box hedges represent a music staff and the flowering roses the notes.

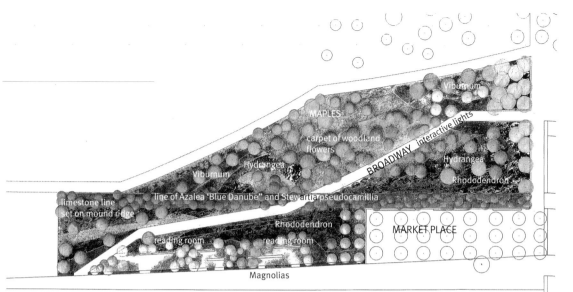

Viburnum

MAPLES

carpet of woodland flowers

BROADWAY interactive lights

Hydrangea

Hydrangea

Viburnum

Rhododendron

limestone line set on mound ridge

line of Azalea "Blue Danube" and Stewartia pseudocamillia

Rhododendron

MARKET PLACE

reading room   reading room

Magnolias

CENTRAL AXIS

Broadway is a more irregular path than the central axis, and is paved with black slate gravel. It runs from the northern plaza to the sculpture field, passing on its way over two wooded hills and between the Gasholder Ponds. At night, as you walk along the Broadway you are accompanied by the illumination of an interactive light sculpture.

Night-time public safety in the park is enhanced by an interactive **lighting plan**. Photoelectric sensors placed alongside the Broadway respond to the proximity of pedestrians, making use of the path visible from afar.

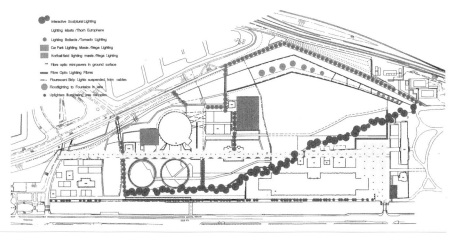

While Gustafson set to work elaborating the park design, Francine Houben of the architecture firm Mecanoo was asked to prepare a master plan. This plan defines the general principles for both the newbuild and the renovation of the existing buildings. One of its main objectives is to intermesh the development planning of the buildings and the park, so as to generate a harmony of activities and atmosphere between the inside and the outside of the buildings.

Houben achieved the intermeshing, as mentioned earlier, by designating a number of different zones within the Westergasfabriek, including The Village, The Childrens' Village, The Spectacle Village and *Cité des Arts*. Each of these zones has different functions and a distinct atmosphere. As to the buildings, an important principle was that their industrial origins had to remain visible, without them being restored to their exact former state. The master plan uses keywords like robustness, simplicity, contrast and freedom to make sure the park and the buildings speak the same 'language'. It also stipulates that the building

SeARCH / Bjarne Mastenbroek
Korfball association clubhouse and changing rooms

The changing rooms and showers are planned on the ground floor of the Transformer Building. Current ideas tend towards a detached unit occupying one quarter of the so-called 'hall of pillars'.

The clubhouse proper will be in the Ladderhouse, which will have to be extended for this purpose. The original design was for an underground extension, but remnants of foundations and the polluted soil at this spot made it impractical. A compact annexe is now proposed on one side. In the original Ladderhouse, the sketch design shows a freestanding cylindrical volume containing the toilets, the kitchen, the storeroom and the bar.

interiors must be kept as spacious as possible and so do justice to the unique character of the buildings.

Whereas Gustafson was challenged to set an explicit personal stamp on the open space of the Westergasfabriek, a much more restrained approach has been required for the buildings. The Mecanoo master plan describes a renovation that serves two goals. Firstly, the architectural quality of the buildings must be brought to the fore or repaired. Secondly, the buildings must be adapted for their future designated use. The only newbuild elements of the project are to be the *Cité des Arts*, the annexe to the Gasholder and the extension of the Ladderhouse on behalf of the korfball association.

The restraint has partly been for financial reasons. Besides, it is Gosschalk's original nineteenth-century architecture that is meant claim the visitor's attention, not the work done by today's architects. Francine Houben was initially appointed as the project supervisor, with her firm Mecanoo also undertaking conversion of the Gasholder, the Transformer Building and the Purifier Building. But in the course of the project, as it became clear that the bulk of the work would consist of preserving and refurbishing the existing structures rather than adding new elements, Houben agreed with MAB to hand over her supervisory task to a restoration specialist.

The real estate developer MAB and the district opted for Braaksma & Roos, an architecture firm renowned for restoration work (their most noteworthy project being Berlage's Gemeentemuseum in The Hague). Yske Braaksma, as the new supervisor, acted as an intermediary between the designers and the official committees for building aesthetics (*Welstand*) and historic buildings (*Monumenten*). After the withdrawal of Mecanoo, it was still necessary to take a number of important design decisions, in particular affecting the renovation of the Purifier Building, the Transformer building and the service spaces of the Gasholder. Braaksma received a number of specific commissions for these parts of the project, and was able to elaborate on the preliminary designs prepared by Mecanoo.

The other architects for the Westergasfabriek have been N2 architekten (for the new buildings of the *Cité des Arts* and a series of smaller buildings), including the Regulator House and the Machine Building) and the firm SeARCH of Bjarne Mastenbroek (for the clubhouse and changing rooms of the korfball association). At the time of writing of this book, the designs are at various stages of completion. The plans reproduced here should therefore not be taken as representing the final situation.

While everyone can now admire the layout of the new park, and soon the renovated buildings too, it is hoped that the third main component of the Westergasfabriek project will leave no visible traces whatsoever. This has not made the task of the ground cleanup any less urgent. Getting the soil pollution

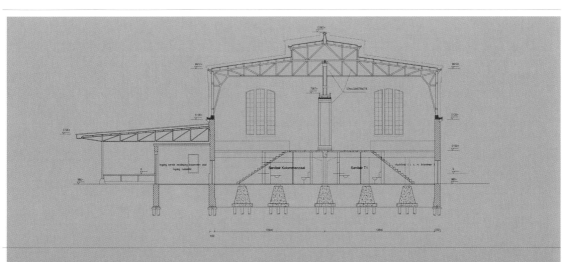

Braaksma & Roos
Renovation of Purification Building and Transformer Building; extension of Gasholder

The firm of Braaksma & Roos has itself undertaken the tasks of renovating the Transformer Building and designing the extension to the Gasholder. The firm is also completing the Purifier Building renovation plans, which still had a number of gaps when they took over the project. The building services, for example, will be better integrated, and the regular rhythm of openings in the long facades will be restored as far as possible – the original regularity was impaired over the years due to the replacement of many of the window units and the construction of doors in various places. A complete reconstruction of the original facade layout is out of the question, but localized repairs and the application of well-chosen colours will moderate the most disturbing deviations. The main change will be the addition of canopies to the long facades (the Purifier Building had these in its original state). The new canopies, with contemporary styling, will function as a unifying element to counteract the irregularities of the lower facades. They will also create a transitional zone between the outside and inside.

The brief for the Transformer Building focuses on restoring the shell of the building. The detailed plan will impair the spatial quality of the interior as little as possible. In the (newer) north wing, the ground floor will accommodate the changing rooms of the korfball association (to a design by SeARCH); the first floor can be divided up into flexible units. The older part will be a flexible space which could be used as a theatre, for example. There is room between the older part and the north wing for a catering amenity.

Structural repairs to the Gasholder are now complete, but an extension is still needed for functions that cannot be accommodated inside the gasholder itself. The provisional design shows these functions housed in three satellites shaped as segments of circles, spaced at a distance of four metres from the outer wall. The first satellite is the entrance pavilion, and the second contains public spaces such as toilets and a lounge. The third satellite houses artists' facilities such as dressing rooms and a green room. The satellites will have a steel skeleton with extensive glazing. The projections connecting the satellites to the Gasholder are of glass, so that the new structures will seem detached from the main volume.

N2 architekten
Cité des Arts, renovation of existing buildings

The firm N2 architekten has been commissioned for the renovation of some ten of the smaller buildings and for the newbuild of *Cité des Arts*. The renovation plans aim primarily at relieving the old buildings as far as possible of later additions. For buildings which formerly contained machinery, this means keeping only the outer walls and the roofs. Items that need to be added to the buildings, such as a pantry or toilet group, will be designed as far as possible as freestanding elements, detached from the original structure. In other buildings, such as the Supervisor's Houses, the non-loadbearing walls will be demolished.

Planned in the Regulator House at the main entrance to the Westergasfabriek, are the information and ticket counter (ground floor) and the offices of the management company (in the attic storey). Here, too, the original spatial quality of the interior will be restored as far as possible. Interior walls added later will be demolished. The Regulator House will gain two new, contemporary entrances, which will transect the historic building in such a way that they will effectively conduct visitors straight through the ticket office into the Westergasfabriek grounds.

For the *Cité des Arts*, the existing situation will impose a number of constraints. Around the distribution station, which will remain in place in the middle of this location, there is a zone of 25 metres where a maximum of fifty people may occupy a given building at any one time. There are also restrictions on the functions of buildings lying in this zone. The ground moreover contains a tangle of buried pipes and conduits, above which building is forbidden. Eight new buildings will be appended to two smaller old buildings, Regulator House 2 and the Ammonia Boilerhouse. They have been designed to some extent as a single object, with right-angled and diagonal incisions. The direction of the angled faces is determined by the courses of the underground pipes and by the shape of the plan area. These lines are prolonged in other places. The tilted shape of the zinc roofs gives the upper floors striking height differences from front to back. The outer walls are clad in varnished wood. The bay dimension of 7.2 metres is not legible in the continuous fenestration strips.

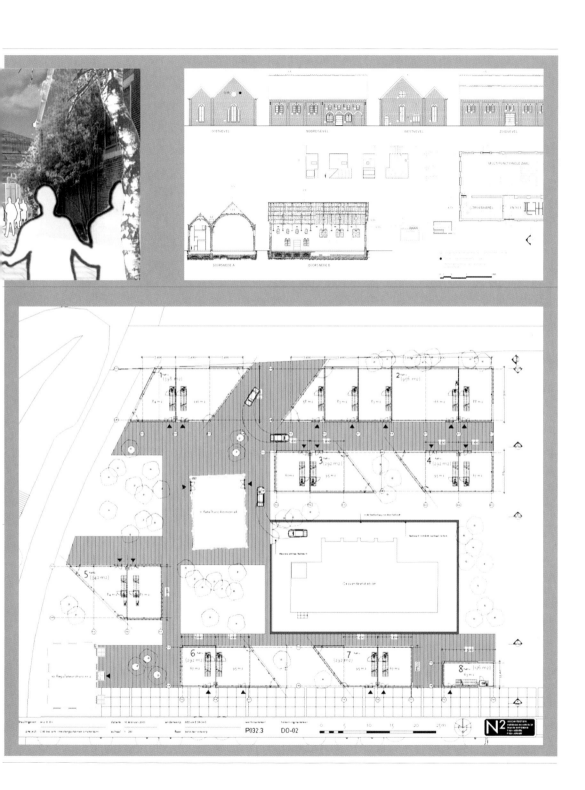

under control was, after all, a mandatory precondition for construction of the park and for assigning the buildings a public function.

Had the regulations of the nineteen eighties still be applicable, the whole project would have been impossible. The government decided then that soil cleanup operations must, in cases of serious pollution, always be 'multi-functional'. In other words, the decontaminated area had to be made suitable for any conceivable function. In the case of the Westergasfabriek, this would have meant excavating and hauling away all the contaminated soil. Not only would that have been impossibly expensive, but nowhere could conceivably have been found to dump the polluted spoils.

So it was fortunate that standards had considerably eased by the period of development planning for the Westergasfabriek. The main instigator of this policy change was the director of the Amsterdam Environmental Department. Jan Cleij had become convinced during the eighties that the nationally prescribed regulations were virtually impossible to work with. The insistence on multi-functional cleanups necessitated such vast expenditures that there would never be enough money available to clean up even a proportion of the country's pollution hot spots. The regulations had moreover been based on the arguable assumption that soil pollution was concentrated into a limited number of places. In actuality, the soil is polluted throughout Amsterdam. Satisfying the national requirements would have meant, for example, demolishing the whole of the *Jordaan* quarter in order to decontaminate the ground beneath it. The supposed pollution hot spots proved, on further study, to be individual peaks in a pattern of pollution that stretched all over the city.

One of Cleij's achievements was to convince the Amsterdam City Council of the importance of 'function-oriented cleanups'. In contrast to multi-functional decontamination, the measures to be taken in function-oriented soil treatment vary according to the intended future use. Two criteria apply: people must not run a risk of coming into contact with the pollution, and the pollutants must not seep farther in the groundwater. These more realistic criteria produce a substantial reduction of costs. For a project like the Westergasfabriek, the necessary investments was only one tenth of the amount that would have been required for a multi-functional cleanup.

The Westergasfabriek is one of the first large projects for which plans were developed on the basis of functional decontamination. This starting point led to a simple solution: the function of a park implied that visitors must not come into contact with the pollution. No particular measures were required to achieve this in the paved areas, and elsewhere the polluted soil had to be covered by a layer of clean topsoil. Depending on the local situation, the topsoil layer varies from 50 cm to 1 metre in thickness. The buildings had to be given vapour proof floors. The seepage of pollutants to the surroundings could be prevented by encircling the site with a barrier of sheetpiling.

It was not always possible to maintain the simplicity of this approach in the detailing of the cleanup plan. Gustafson's park design is, for example, not

The site during the soil cleanup

two-dimensional but three-dimensional. At some points the ground was excavated – to create the pools, for instance – and the spoils were used to create raised areas elsewhere on the site. In collaboration with the design firm of Gustafson and Porter, the British engineering group Ove Arup prepared a plan to carry out that work as efficiently as possible. Further awkward complications arose during the implementation phase. Unexpectedly high levels of pollution were encountered during the excavation of soil to make the pools in the foundations of the former retort house.

A more serious setback manifested itself when the concrete roof of one of the two water-filled gasholder foundations was being broken open to create the Gasholder Ponds. A cloud of foul-smelling vapour rose as the pieces of concrete fell into the sludge below. The sludge proved to contain unexpectedly high concentrations of polluting chemicals. On the insistence of local residents' organizations, the Minister of Housing, Spatial Planning and the Environment, Mr. Pronk, decided personally that the contaminated sludge would have to be removed, even though the City Environment Department thought a covering layer would have been adequate. The ministerial decision meant departing from the principle of a 'closed soil balance', in which soil would be displaced only from one place to another within the site, in this particular case.

Now that the soil cleanup has been completed, everyone can use the site for its intended purpose – to work or recreate there – without encountering risks from pollution. Blocking potential seepage from the site with a barrier of sheetpiling can be put off for a while. Regular measurements take place in the vicinity of the Westergasfabriek to determine whether the soil pollution is spreading, and as yet the situation appears to be stable. So phase 2 of the cleanup (the construction of the sheetpiling barrier) is no longer classed as urgent.

Conditions for a suc

At least two kinds of condition have to be met to succeed in a project like the Westergasfabriek. The previous chapter focussed on conditions of the first kind – on the visions and concepts, on the designs and plans – in short, on the *substance* of the project. Conditions of the second kind are just as important, though. They relate to the *process* that makes it possible to develop those plans and concepts and then carry them out in practice.

To the outside world, this is one of the less visible aspects of the Westergasfabriek project – and rightly so. The public image of the Westergasfabriek must be one of a hive of cultural activity, going on in and around historic industrial buildings in a brand new park. It should not be an image of the small group of people who guided the project to fruition, working from a tiny office – first in one of the Supervisors' Houses, and then in a Portakabin. Now the work of the project team is finished, all that remains are the archives and a bunch of memories.

The process may have reached its end but it was perhaps the most critical aspect of the enterprise. The substance of most plans is in a certain sense interchangeable. A different planned use could just as easily have inspired the revival of the Westergasfabriek. And, other things being equal, if the competition for the park design had yielded a different winner, the outcome would have simply been a different park. The process by which all this happened has had much less scope for variation. As in comparable projects elsewhere, the Westergasfabriek demonstrates that the structure and the management of the process are crucial.

Temporary accommodation for the Westergasfabriek Project Office

ssful transformation

The first requirement is that the process must be open-ended and flexible. It was clear from the start that the uncertainties would outweigh the certainties in the Westergasfabriek project. When the buildings were first made available for cultural uses (initially for one year only) in late 1992, the purpose was to turn the Westergasfabriek as quickly as possible into a place of some significance, and to prevent the buildings falling into the hands of unintended users – a fate which would have severely hampered the implementation of new plans. A definitive new use had not yet been authorized. Money had scarcely been discussed, and it was still necessary to build up a relationship with local residents. All that existed was a sketchy idea about the direction in which development of the Westergasfabriek should go. The grounds were to be added to urban district's public space, and the buildings were to have a public function. What that function would be was not yet defined; nor was the design of the open space, nor how to deal with the soil pollution problem.

The fact that a concrete end-picture had not yet been formed at that juncture did not exclude setting the process in motion. Step by step, the original uncertainties were eradicated, but each step raised new uncertainties of its own. An open-ended, flexible process was the only way to respond adequately to this situation. It was also important not fall into the trap of imagining the process to be simpler and less ambiguous than it was, of reasoning from a defined, concrete target situation. Obviously there was a picture of the direction in which the process had to move, and of a final result which was slowly but surely becoming clear. The park design, for example, developed from a set of broad principles, via a more detailed functional brief and a number of competition entries, to the choice of a landscape architect, who then prepared a provisional and eventually a definitive design. At each stage, unexpected situations emerged which posed questions that could not be answered.

This open-ended manner of management is the best way to steer processes which are subject to so many uncertain factors that the outcome is highly unpredictable. A process of this kind has to correct its course continually and find solutions for unexpected problems. It is the opposite of what may be termed a *linear* process – a process suited to standard situations, in which action can be taken on the basis of predefined procedures. That is the way housing estates and roads are built, and the way the garbage is collected.

The linear approach is normal in a bureaucracy. In the standard procedure for building projects developed in Amsterdam in the nineteen-eighties, each phase is exactly defined. The project starts with a 'strength/weakness analysis', and this is followed by a 'memorandum of starting points', a 'schedule of requirements' etc. This kind of procedure is no doubt fine for projects that are not too complicated and are predictable. It is however impractical for a complicated enterprise like the Westergasfabriek, however, which is really three projects in one (the ground cleanup, the park and the buildings).

For the Westergasfabriek it was therefore crucial to avoid strictly linear models and operate according to principles of process management. That is not to say there were not, within the overall process, countless sub-processes for which a linear approach was appropriate. On the contrary, regular, linear procedures and methods were followed all the time. The design of the park went impeccably through the customary phases, from design concept, via provisional design to a definitive design, and permits were applied for following the standard Amsterdam procedures. Process management does not mean throwing the rules and procedures overboard; what it does mean is putting all the linear sub-processes in control of a management team which has enough flexibility to respond to the unexpected.

As a concrete example, people first assumed that the three main subprojects – the cleaning up the soil, building the park and restoring the buildings – would take place more or less in parallel. The components would have been ideally integrated that way. But a number of setbacks put both the buildings and the soil cleanup well behind schedule. Since the design and construction of the park proceeded relatively smoothly, the park started getting ahead of the other two subprojects. Due to force of circumstances, the park thus took the lead, and the other two subprojects had to adjust themselves to it in various respects. Process management is indispensable in situations like this to enable an effective response to changing circumstances.

Process management thus means working towards a goal which is not yet certain. It is a working method which has been widely adopted by large software companies like Microsoft. The development of software often begins while only the rough direction is known but there is as yet no well-defined end product. The precise nature of the product crystallizes out in the course of the development process itself. The moment it is launched on the market may also be arbitrary: in that case the product represents only the current state of the art. This approach differs fundamentally from that of traditional industries where product development is geared to a well-defined end product. In this respect, too, the Westergasfabriek has become an unintentional emblem of the transition from the industrial to the post-industrial city.

The process management approach does place particular demands on the people who work on the project. They have to cope with situations in which they cannot fall back on established rules and well-tried recipes. They must be people who thrive in situations of uncertainty, and who come into their own when their creativity is put to the test.

Evert Verhagen

The second precondition for the successful development of the Westergasfabriek has already been touched on briefly, and it is a consequence of the first.
It is that, from the viewpoint of the project team, the project process is more
important than the substance of the project. In a situation where the goal is
liable to change at any time, the quality of the process management creates
the conditions needed for integration and continuity. As an example, the competition for the park design yielded five concepts, each of which might equally
have been chosen as the basis for the actual design. By taking a position of
professional indifference towards what the park would eventually look like, the
project team left itself free to go further with whichever of the five candidates
would be chosen.

For the same reason, it was deliberately decided not to include designers
or engineers in the project team, despite the project being one with an emphasis
on the making of plans and on executing them. The project bureau always
aimed to be a small, versatile organization without extreme specialists. The first
staff member of the project manager Evert Verhagen (who himself studied
hydrological engineering) was Fred Goedbloed, a historian; but he could just as
well have been a classicist or a social geographer. Rather than specialist knowledge, membership of the project team called for broader abilities – managerial
talent, a capacity to harmonize processes and, above all, excellent communicative skills.

The management of communication was, from the outset, the most
important task – and the main instrument – of the project bureau. This was
true at all phases and levels of the process. Communication was essential for
spreading the vision for the new future of the Westergasfabriek, and also for the
day-to-day task of coordinating the subprocesses. Good communication is all
the more important when a project team cannot resort to formal authorization
in every circumstance. The team was admittedly delegated a number of import-

One of the workshops held
during park development
planning

Exhibition of the park plan

Kathryn Gustafson presenting
the provisional design

Pieter den Boeft,
Kathryn Gustafson,
Evert Verhagen
and Ruud Grondel

Presentation of the park design
to local residents

ant powers by the urban district's regular officialdom, but these powers were often insufficient to give them the clout to get things done. This kind of limitation is something we also observe in e.g. IBA Emscher Park and Bilbao Ría 2000; the powers granted to the project organizations were in these instances even more limited, among other things because they were not at liberty to commission work from designers. In the case of the Westergasfabriek, the team did have this power, at least for the park.

There is a further (and perhaps even more important) reason for giving prominence to communication. The Westergasfabriek can only be revitalized to become a dynamic spot in the city to the extent that people and organizations are inspired by the project. For residents, tenants, politicians, designers and other partners, the Westergasfabriek has to be the realization of a dream. This is the only way to ensure broad support – and that support is not simply to be had for the asking.

Sometimes the dream was deliberately evoked. In 1996, before a park design existed, Evert Verhagen asked the members of the team then involved in the project to describe their 'dream park'. This aroused a few puzzled looks, but most of them set eagerly to work. The one individual who baulked, ostensibly on the grounds of insufficient expertise, was immediately disqualified in Verhagen's eyes as someone with a great deal to offer the Westergasfabriek. Similar sessions took place at the start of the workshops that followed Kathryn Gustafson's initial design. There, too, the participants had a warm-up session in which they were each asked to talk about their 'dream' park.

Getting people to feel the excitement of the Westergasfabriek was often an important task for the project bureau. Anyone who had dealings with the team was soon cajoled into attending one of the cultural events that took pace on the site during the Interim Use. As a matter of course, lunch would be taken in the West Pacific bar-restaurant; and, at regular intervals, people were bussed

off for a look at IBA Emscher Park, so as to impress them with the surprising atmosphere and possibilities of the defunct mining and industrial complexes.

The normal government apparatus of civil servants is generally ill-equipped to manage major transformations like that of the Westergasfabriek. Creating a special project organization is therefore an obvious step to take. Various models for this organization may be considered. If an important role for private industry such as real estate developers is considered from the outset, the project will often take the form of a public-private partnership – for example, a development company in which both the government and the private sector are represented. It may be that a project is backed by a number of different authorities, and in this case they must all be represented on the steering group of the project.

In comparison, the project organization of the Westergasfabriek was relatively simple. The Westerpark district council took the initiative in the project, and subsequently also took charge of the development process. Other authorities were naturally also concerned with the Westergasfabriek, for example Amsterdam City Council, the Province of North Holland and the national government. But there was no doubt about where the final responsibility lay: with the political administration of the district.

The transfer of the buildings to the real estate development company MAB did not in itself make the project a real example of public-private collaboration. There was no project organization structure in which the district and the developer participated together. Their positions and responsibilities were strictly separate. MAB took charge of the buildings, including responsibility for the business operation within the parameters agreed with the urban district. The district was responsible for the development of the public space (the park) and for the progress of the project as a whole.

Although it never figured as an argument for seeking a real estate developer to deal with the Westergasfabriek buildings, the district's collaboration with MAB had an unforeseen advantage. The mutual obligations proved to have a considerable stabilizing influence on the process. When setbacks occurred, for example the unexpected environmental problems or the general economic downturn, both parties were compelled to keep going with the park and the buildings respectively. This benefit was particularly underscored by the events surrounding the guarantee given by the district to enable the National Restoration Fund's loan to MAB. The negotiations on this were difficult enough, but the eventual conclusion was favourable because neither of the partners could afford to let the whole enterprise founder.

Had that mutual dependency not existed, then it is clear in retrospect that the Westergasfabriek would have suffered the same fate as Amsterdam's Stedelijk Museum, which has been caught in an impasse for some years. A similar interdependency was probably also a factor in the success of Bilbao Ría 2000: the huge number of partners involved in that project may have made its organization extremely complicated, but it did have the effect that once the process was underway none of them could afford to pull out.

Local government councillors involved in the Westergas-fabriek. L. to R.: Dick Jansen, Martine Fransman, Ruud Grondel, Hokon Hansen

A specially formed project team is essential for a project of this scale and complexity. In theory, it might be possible for the project to be conducted by existing governmental structures, but in practice they would quickly get bogged down in questions of official competences and problems of coordination. A project like the Westergasfabriek touches on many different aspects of administration at the same time. Besides spatial planning, it involves the environment, cultural policy, economic development, employment opportunities, resident participation, traffic policy, legal questions and finance.

The existence of a project office does not in any case mean completely sidelining the normal official departments and committees. A small, compact team like that of the Westergasfabriek benefits greatly from the expertise available elsewhere in the official organization. But the project office remains the point where all lines meet, and where any problems arising can be dealt with most efficiently.

Coordination between the various subprocesses and policy areas was not the only reason for creating a project office for the Westergasfabriek project. It was also necessary to make the non-linear process management approach possible. Normal local and national government bodies are used to linear processes; they are generally bureaucracies that follow established procedures to work towards a predefined end-situation. Only a project office that stands outside the normal civil service hierarchy can be flexible enough to improvise and respond effectively to unexpected situations. And only they would have had the stamina to stay the course for thirteen years and so preserve the continuity of the Westergasfabriek project.

The relative autonomy of the Westergasfabriek project office did not mean it was dissociated from the political leadership of the urban district council. But

it implied having a single point of contact, an individual to represent it on the urban district council: a 'portfolio holder', as aldermen of the Amsterdam districts are known. The project team is the direct responsibility of the portfolio holder. The project manager is thus not required to further justify his or her actions to other departments of the district authority or other individual councillors, even when they concern matters covered by their respective portfolios.

It was in fact always a matter of course that redevelopment of the Westergasfabriek would end up in the hands of the urban district and not the city authority of Amsterdam. To start with, the district was the initiator of the project. And although a multimillion euro project like the Westergasfabriek is quite a big undertaking for a district of only 35 thousand inhabitants, it is, in relation to the distribution of departmental competences within Amsterdam local government, clearly a task for the urban district and not for the central city.

In the main, this has proved advantageous. The city government of Amsterdam tends to adopt the form of a many headed monster which expends its energy in discussions with itself, particularly on complex projects. So it can take a long time before a project gets going. Amsterdam has a poor reputation in this respect. It took dozens of years to reach completion of the new city hall (the Stopera), it will be a long wait for completion of the city's new metro line (the Nord-Zuid Line) and, even though budgets of tens of millions of euros were authorized years ago, the refurbishment and extension of the Stedelijk Museum and the Stadsschouwburg are still stuck at the planning stage.

Compared to the city, with its complex organization and the power positions and sectional interests that go along with it, the smaller urban districts are less complex and hence more transparent. It takes less effort in an urban district, both politically and officially, to unite everyone behind a single vision and thus to establish broad support for an ambitious project.

The city of Amsterdam was nonetheless intensively involved in the Westergasfabriek. The size of the investments alone meant that the district could not get by without the aid of the 'central city'. The city also formed a link in the chain leading to the provincial and national governments, which influences various components of the Westergasfabriek project in both policy and financial respects. This was particularly so for the multimillion euro soil cleanup subproject, in which important roles were reserved for the city Environment Department and the Ministry of Housing, Spatial Planning and the Environment.

In 1996, when the Westergasfabriek project began to pick up speed, the urban district decided it was time to ask the central city for support. To avoid the district getting bogged down once again in treacle-like administrative procedures, the city was asked to follow the district's example and appoint a single representative to take responsibility for the project. The 'project alderman' (the city equivalent of the district's 'portfolio holder') had to be more than a coordinator: he would have powers delegated to him from his colleagues on the city

Book launch for 'Een park voor de 21st eeuw' 1998

council insofar as they related to the Westergasfabriek. The project alderman was thus not merely a central point of contact but was in a position to take decisions.

The district reacted somewhat cagily when the city council appointed Edgar Peer as the project alderman. Peer was already the city alderman for economic affairs, while the Westergasfabriek was supposed to be a matter of culture and recreation. There was moreover a difference of political background between Peer, a member of the conservative VVD party, and his negotiating partner on the district council, the *Groen-Links* ('Green Left') portfolio holder Ruud Grondel. The political differences did in fact surface briefly at one point. It was Peer who insisted – initially against the will of the district – on including some newbuild (in the interests of more profitable land use) and on handing over the existing buildings to a private real estate development company. Peer, in other words, wished to give a stronger market emphasis to the project than Grondel first had in mind.

Eventually, the urban district and Peer reached agreement, particularly once he revealed himself to be an enthusiastic supporter of the Westergas-fabriek project on the Amsterdam City Council. Peer was moreover comfortable with the process management approach. He had already exhibited a healthy aversion to procedural obstacles in connection with other large projects in Amsterdam, such as the New Metropolis science museum.

The portfolio holder on the Westerpark District Council nonetheless remained the chief political representative for the Westergasfabriek. After the first initi-atives had been taken under Hokon Hansen, the crucial period of definitive planning commenced under his successor, Ruud Grondel. In 1996, Grondel presented the Development Plan which has since been the main guideline for the whole project. Grondel was followed as portfolio holder for the Westergas-fabriek by Martine Fransman, who was responsible for obtaining perhaps the two most important council decisions: approval of the definitive design for the park, and transfer of the buildings to MAB. Since spring 2001, the portfolio holder for the Westergasfabriek has been Dick Jansen. Much skilled helmsman-ship has been required of Jansen to prevent the project running aground, after the Council of State decree regarding environmental impact reporting.

Although all the portfolio holders for the Westergasfabriek have been Groen-Links members, effort has always been taken to establish the widest possible political support, including support of the opposition parties on the district council. The project has spanned several four-year terms between local elections; it was necessary to prevent the Westergasfabriek from becoming so politicized that it would come up for discussion again every time a new govern-ing coalition was formed.

The relationship between the portfolio holder and the project team, and especially the relationship with project manager Evert Verhagen, is in principle clearly defined. The project manager is a local government officer who, as appropriate to the civil service, is subordinate to a political representative – the portfolio holder, who is in turn answerable to the district council. That a charismatic and inspired man like Verhagen is actually the public face of the Westergasfabriek project does not alter this. He does his job within the space created for him by his portfolio holder.

In everyday practice, the relationship is more complicated. It is precisely because the position of the project manager is such a prominent one that his relationship to his political leadership requires constant adjustment. That implies above all the efficient exchange of information. The project manager, who has been involved with the Westergasfabriek from the start and has seen portfolio holders come and go, inevitably has a considerable head start in knowledge. Only if the project manager provides the portfolio manager with information at relevant moments, is it possible to prevent this knowledge disparity becoming a problem. If the exchange of information were to stagnate, there would be a risk that the portfolio holder's political answerability would become a farce, and the project manager might well run off with the project – after which he would probably fall flat, together with the project, owing to the lack of political backing.

In the case of the Westergasfabriek, the unequivocal character of that relation has never been in danger. There were however some energetic confrontations between Verhagen and his portfolio holder, particularly in the Grondel period, when the most important decisions had to be made. On looking back, they now argue that it would have been a worrying sign if they had not had a tussle of words now and then. Getting a project of that kind underway needs people with an outspoken vision, and the self-willed character that goes along with that is bound to result in an occasional clash.

While on the one hand the process must be rooted in the governmental body, which acts as the initiator and commissioning client, on the other links must be established and maintained with other groups who are of critical importance to the success of the project. Of these groups, which include the users of the buildings, the most important have always been the residents of the adjoining neighbourhoods (Spaandammerbuurt and Staatsliedenbuurt) and their organizations.

It is after all due to the residents' endeavours over dozens of years that a park has been created on the Westergasfabriek grounds. The park is in the first place *their* park, and it was inconceivable that they would be left out of the process that led to its creation. Moreover, the success of projects to transform brownfield sites depends on the extent to which the new designated use is rooted in the direct surroundings. In the case of IBA Emscher Park, Landschaftspark Duisburg-Nord has become a much more vital place than the Zollverein XII project in Essen, where a design centre is being developed which has scarcely any connection with local residents.

As to the Westergasfabriek, public support among local residents has provided some necessary momentum at crucial junctures. This was true, for example, for the involvement of the then director of the city Environment Department, Jan Cleij. His application, and his willingness to conceive unconventional solutions for the soil decontamination problems, followed only after the residents' convincing him that Staatsliedenbuurt and Spaandammerbuurt had a desperate shortage of green areas.

It was thus evident that the project team and the residents' groups needed each other. This is not to say the relationship was always free of problems. Periods of fruitful collaboration alternated with periods marked by distrust and dispute. Now, at the time of completion of the park, the atmosphere prevailing between the urban district council and the Friends of the Westerpark is far from ideal. Their differences centre around the implementation of the decree of the Council of State, who have decided that an environmental impact report is needed for the new zoning plan.

When there were clashes between the residents' organizations and the district, or – more specifically – between the Friends of the Westerpark and the project team, they were often about the influence of the residents' organizations on the decision-making process. That influence was sometimes arranged to everyone's satisfaction; for example, in the selection of the park architect, and in the preparation of the provisional design (about which more later). But the project team sometimes drew a line – for example when putting an end to the involvement of the residents' organizations in the detailed design of the park. Once the main outlines of the design had been settled, the project manager decided that the landscape architect Gustafson must have full freedom of scope. She must not be burdened with consulting with the Friends on matters like the selection of plants or materials. However, the residents' organizations could not resign themselves to a position in which were informed of progress but no longer had any influence on the design process.

Sometimes, too, differences arose on more substantive matters. The residents' organizations held that the Westergasfabriek site should become a park for the benefit of people in the direct surroundings. They had come to accept that the buildings would be given a cultural function, but that function must not be to the detriment of the possibilities of using the park. They wanted less 'stone' and more 'green', and feared that large public events would cause nuisance to the local residents. Agreement was often reached in such cases; for example, the park gained a greater area of greenery and less of pavement in the course of the design process, and the number of large public events held on the Events Field was restricted to six per annum. But the conflict was not always as easily resolved. When the urban district and the Province of North Holland stood their ground in arguing that no environmental impact report was required for the new zoning plan, it was the residents' organizations who took their case to the Council of State.

Local residents demonstrating
during a council session

In times when the relation between the urban district and the residents' organizations was poor, their mutual perceptions deteriorated accordingly. The project team found the Friends of the Westerpark an exasperating group, who besides being intransigent were not even representative of all the local residents. The question pending in the background was who should be considered the real representative of the neighbourhoods. From an activist viewpoint, that was the residents' organizations, whereas the district council argued that it was the democratically elected representative of the local population. Conversely, the Friends and related organizations accused the district more than once of trying to make the Westergasfabriek into a prestige project and of losing sight of the residents' interests. They also disapproved of selling the buildings to a private real estate developer, who in their view would be interested only in earning as much money as possible on the deal.

Against this, as said, there were periods in which the involvement of the organized residents took the concrete form of successful collaboration. This was particularly true in the phase of defining the design brief for the park, followed by the selection of a landscape architect. It started with project manager Verhagen requesting the Friends of the Westerpark to make the first move, by setting down ten principle wishes. The result was a text which filled no more than a single page, and which then formed the basis for defining the formal schedule of requirements of the new park.

To select the landscape architect, the project team formed a 'park working group'. It included three representatives of the residents' organizations and representatives of among others the tenants of the buildings, the urban district and the City Monuments Department. In the first round, each member of the committee was allowed to put forward a candidate, resulting in a longlist of over a hundred names. An elimination round followed in which each member of the

'Ideeën ontruim je niet'
('You can't evict ideas')

working group nominated three designers so as to leave roughly thirty potential candidates, who were then requested to send information on their work. Out of the thirty, twelve landscape architects were then selected and invited to make a twenty-minute presentation. This made it possible to judge the designers directly for their communicative capacities – a quality that the project team considered of the greatest importance.

The last task of the working group was to select five of the twelve landscape architects to be invited to participate in a limited competition. It had been decided beforehand that, if the working group failed to reach agreement at this stage, the residents' representatives would be allowed to nominate two of the five candidates; but this recourse proved unnecessary.

For the competition itself, a committee of judges was appointed, once again including two representatives of the residents. This procedure too proceeded quickly and without serious problems. Before the five park concepts were published, the Friends of the Westerpark had a further opportunity to make their views known to the judging committee. *De Staatskrant*, a normally critical local newspaper produced by the residents' organizations, subsequently published a strikingly favourable opinion on the working method and the outcome.

The residents' organizations retained a voice in the plan development for a period after Kathryn Gustafson had won the competition and was commissioned to design the park. In the detailing of certain components during the first phase of development, the project team set a high value on a broad-based contribution from as many as possible of those involved, and it was taken for granted that these included the residents. A number of workshops were held in 1998 on topics such as ecology, public events and traffic. The Friends of the Westerpark were also represented in the group supervising the landscape architect's work towards the definitive design. This group was given the rather unfortunate title of the 'design team', which gave the impression that its members could as it were take part in the actual designing. But, as said, that was something that project manager Verhagen definitely wished to avoid: the design work must be left to the professional designers of the Gustafson-Porter firm. Achieving a good design would be inconceivable if the designer were forced to share the responsibility with others. It was expected, of course, that Gustafson would intermittently submit her ideas to the experts – among whom the residents were also counted. However, the final decision had to remain with the designer. The only aspect that others, including not only the residents' organizations but the project team, might take a hand in was the *programme*, and that was settled by the definitive design.

The development company MAB also had no more than a marginal influence on the park design. Ensuring the best possible match between the functions of the buildings and those of the park was a dealt with in the master plan for the Westergasfabriek site, prepared by Francine Houben (who, as mentioned, collaborated with Gustafson on the winning park design).

The project team's relations with the residents' organizations were not the only ones that were sometimes problematic – for example relations with the tenants of the buildings and with MAB. The project management did not always back away from such conflicts. Anyone trying to bring such an ambitious project as the Westergasfabriek to fruition must be to some extent convinced of his or her views and must remain so. Self-will goes along with passion for the project, and whoever choses this path knows in advance that this can invoke resistance. If concessions were made to all the wishes of those concerned, ranging from the Dutch Railways to the city departments, or from the union of cyclists to local dog owners, eventually nothing would be left of the park.

The project management decided that although there was no taboo on compromises, these must never work to the detriment of the clarity and direction of the design process: a good design depends on the professional skills of the designer and can thus never be an outcome of haggling over design outlooks and principles. When the residents called for more greenery and Gustafson responded by giving the sculpture garden grass instead of paving as she first proposed, she did not do so for the sake of peace and quiet, but because she considered it an improvement. This relatively uncompromising attitude was typical of the whole development process and it contributed strongly to its success.

A measured reluctance to compromise must be matched by determination to reach consensus in the end – this may seem paradoxical, but it is not. It is through protectiveness towards the quality of the process, and unwillingness compromise it for the sake of short-term success, that a final result has been achieved of which everyone can feel proud.

Colophon

Final editing Olof Koekebakker and
Projectbureau Westergasfabriek:
Evert Verhagen, Marieke Wiersma

Copy editing Els Brinkman

Translation Victor Joseph

Design Frank Beekers

Lithography and printing SSP,
Amsterdam

Production Anneloes van der Leun

Publisher Simon Franke

This publication was made possible by the Netherlands
Architecture Fund.

© NAi Publishers, Rotterdam, 2003

Available in North, South and Central America through
D.A.P./Distributed Art Publishers Inc, 155 Sixth Avenue
2nd Floor, New York, NY 10013-1507, Tel 212 6271999,
Fax 212 6279484.

Available in the United Kingdom and Ireland through Art
Data, 12 Bell Industrial Estate, 50 Cunnington Street,
London W4 5HB, Tel 208 7471061, Fax 208 7422319.

Photography
ARCHIEF WESTERGASFABRIEK 12, 14, 18, 25
(bottom), 26/27, 28, 29, 30, 36 (top), 52,
54, 55, 58, 66, 78, 79, 80 (centre left,
centre right and bottom), 81 (centre left
and centre right), 82 (top), 127, 134, 135,
141 (bottom)
• AVEQ FOTOGRAFIE 37
• FRANK BEEKERS 19, 93 (centre), 95
• BILBAO RÍA 2000 15, 16, 17
• CARO BONINK 9
• © GRAND-HORNU IMAGES – CLICHÉ
ETIENNE WATELET 20
• JEROEN HILAK 61, 80 (top), 81 (bottom),
82 (bottom)
• IBA EMSCHER PARK 12
• JANNES LINDERS 21 (centre), 85, 86/87,
88/89, 90, 91, 92, 96, 97, 99, 100, 101,
102, 104, 118
• MASS MoCA (MASSACHUSETTS MUSEUM
OF CONTEMPORARY ART) 21 (top)
• JOSÉ MELO 34, 39 (top and bottom left),
43 (left), 132, 133, 139, 141 (top)
• KATRIEN MULDER 94, 106, 107, 108, 109,
110/111, 112, 113, 114, 115, 116, 117, 119
• DE PONT STICHTING VOOR HEDENDAAGSE
KUNST, TILBURG 21 (centre)
• SIEBE SWART 11
• TATE MODERN 22 (bottom)
• ARJEN VELDT 36 (bottom), 39 (centre and
bottom right), 40, 41, 42, 43 (right), 44,
45, 46, 47, 48, 49, 60, 62, 63, 64, 65, 67,
128, 130, 138/139
• HANNES WALLRAFEN 35, 56
• from: Catalogus *Secret Dreams*, Wild
Vlees, Amsterdam 131
• from: Kees Zomer, Paul Lankamp,
*Westergasfabriek, het terrein en de
gebouwen, een cultuurhistorische
verkenning*, Bureau Monumentenzorg,
Amsterdam 1998 22, 23, 24, 25 (top)
• from: L. Zwiers, *IJzerconstructies*,
Amsterdam 1916 24 (bottom right)

NAi Publishers is an internationally orientated publisher specialized in developing,
producing and distributing books on architecture, visual arts and related disciplines.
www.naipublishers.nl
Printed and bound in the Netherlands

ISBN 90-5662-339-7